LOGICAL BRIDGE PLAY

HUGH KELSEY

LONDON
VICTOR GOLLANCZ LTD
in association with
Peter Crawley
1988

First published in 1976
by Faber & Faber Ltd

First paperback edition published in 1988
by Victor Gollancz Ltd
14 Henrietta Street, London WC2E 8QJ

British Library Cataloguing in Publication Data
Kelsey, Hugh
  Logical bridge play.
  1. Contract bridge
  I. Title
  795.41'5   GV1282.3

  ISBN 0–575–04138–2

Printed in Great Britain by
WBC Bristol and Maesteg

Contents

Acknowledgements

As ever, I am indebted to my good friend
Denis Young for eliminating a number of
errors of grammar, analysis and style. I tend
to chafe a bit when the typescript comes
back accompanied by fifty foolscap pages of
criticism that is always blunt and often
downright impertinent. But I am well aware
that the end product is a better book.

H.W.K.

Introduction

The brilliant card player achieves his results through a combination of logic and flair. To the beginner, watching the deep finesses succeed and the singleton kings drop as if by magic, the proportion appears to be nine parts of flair to one of logic. The more experienced player with some knowledge of the lines of thought involved might estimate the mixture to be made up of equal parts of logic and flair. The expert may be happy to encourage such illusions, but in his heart he knows that flair accounts for no more than a tiny fraction of his success. His game is based almost entirely on logic.

Flair is a quality that cannot be taught, for it is largely a matter of instinct, closely allied to what is known as 'table presence'. Every great player has this attribute, a heightened awareness of all that goes on at the table and a super-sensitivity to the mannerisms and reactions of his opponents. Thus a vibration that appears slightly out of true may lead the master to the winning line of play, even when it is against the odds.

What can be taught are the simple processes of reasoning by which apparently miraculous results are achieved. The real secret of the expert is his ability to make logic seem like flair.

In setting out my examples I have kept to the quiz format, showing only two hands and inviting the reader to tackle the problem himself before going on to read the solution. This may reduce the entertainment value of the book in the eyes of those who dislike being put to work. But, as always, I am aiming at the keen player who wishes to improve his game, and this purpose is best served by reproducing the conditions that obtain at the bridge table.

1. Magic Numbers

Those who are weak in mathematics have no reason to shy away from the title. Bridge is not a mathematical game and it would be a waste of time to bring a slide-rule or an electronic calculator to the table with you. There may be one or two mathematicians in the ranks of the top experts, but there are many more lawyers, doctors, teachers, musicians and other upright citizens who would not recognize a mathematical proposition if it stared them in the face.

Mathematics can be dispensed with, but a little basic arithmetic is needed at the bridge table. This is because much of the logic we use is based on arithmetical factors. The arithmetic is of elementary-school standard, involving no more than the adding or subtracting of a few figures. You already do as much in the auction when you add up your points to see if you have an opening bid. In almost universal use today is the point count devised by the late Milton Work (ace—4, king—3, queen—2, knave—1). This is a simple and reasonably accurate method of evaluating a bridge hand, and it is rare for a player to make a mistake in totalling his points.

Players go astray not in doing their sums but in making proper use of the answers. It is not always appreciated, for instance, that the value of counting points extends beyond the bidding. Good players harness the Milton Work count during the play of the hand as well, applying it in the light of the opponents' bidding (or lack of bidding) to figure out the position of key cards.

The first magic number we are going to consider is thirteen, for this represents the number of high-card points on which a player will (almost infallibly) open the bidding. From an opponent's failure to open the bidding much can be deduced. The arguments are simple, but it may help those unaccustomed to the lines of reasoning involved if we break them down into their component parts and examine them in detail. This entails a brief excursion into the field of logic.

Francis Bacon described logic as 'a kind of athletic art to strengthen the sinews of the understanding'. It has long been recognized that, no matter what the subject under study, a course in logic can serve as a valuable discipline, acting as a mental tonic and helping to develop precision of thought. This is a quality that bridge players need to cultivate above all else, since hazy thinking is incompatible with good bridge.

The principles of logic have hardly changed since they were first defined by Aristotle some twenty-three centuries ago. The logical argument most commonly used at the bridge table is the hypothetical syllogism. This may be set out formally as follows:

Major premiss—If West had held thirteen high-card points he would have opened the bidding.

Minor premiss—He did not open the bidding.

Conclusion   —Therefore he does not have thirteen high-card points.

Naturally we are not aware of going through each stage of the argument in our minds. That would be altogether too laborious a procedure. In speaking or writing about the matter we would normally shorten the argument to the form known as an enthymeme—that is a syllogism in which one of the premisses is suppressed. We would say something like: 'I knew that West could not have thirteen points since he failed to open the bidding.'

The actual mental process by which we arrive at the conclusion does not require the argument to be put into words at all. Indeed, the situation is so familiar and our reaction so automatic that the conclusion materializes without any conscious thought on our part. This is accomplished in the fraction of a micro-second that it takes for an electronic impulse to travel a few centimetres across the brain.

It is just as well that no great effort is involved, for there may be a lot more to be done before we are rewarded with any real indication of how to play the hand. The next step is to take our first conclusion and put it to work as the major premiss of a new syllogism. After the play of a couple of tricks, for example, we may be in a position to continue:

Major premiss—West does not have thirteen high-card points.

Minor premiss—He is known to have the ace of spades and the king and queen of hearts.

Conclusion —Therefore he does not have four more points.

The logical chain is extended link by link. Taking the argument a stage further and starting from the basic premiss that West does not have four more points, it is a simple matter to infer that East must have any ace that is outstanding. At this point we have reached a conclusion that may be of genuine help in the play of the hand.

Here is an example of the practical application of this sort of reasoning.

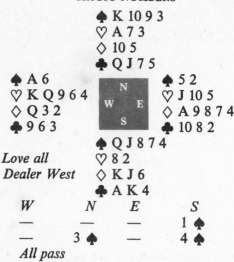

♠ K 10 9 3
♡ A 7 3
◇ 10 5
♣ Q J 7 5

♠ A 6   ♠ 5 2
♡ K Q 9 6 4   ♡ J 10 5
◇ Q 3 2   ◇ A 9 8 7 4
♣ 9 6 3   ♣ 10 8 2

♠ Q J 8 7 4
Love all   ♡ 8 2
Dealer West   ◇ K J 6
♣ A K 4

W	N	E	S
—	—	—	1 ♠
—	3 ♠	—	4 ♠

All pass

West leads the king of hearts and is allowed to hold the
first trick. When East encourages with the knave West continues with the six of hearts to dummy's ace. A spade is led to
the queen and ace, and West leads a third heart for South to
ruff. A trump to the king draws the remaining trumps, and
the declarer is left with the task of avoiding two diamond
losers in order to make his contract.

Well, those who have followed the arguments on the pre-
vious page will realize that there is no real problem. West,
who passed originally, has already shown up with the ace of
spades and the king and queen of hearts. East is therefore
marked with the ace of diamonds, and South should put up
the king if East plays low.

Thus what might appear to the hazy thinker to be a guess
in diamonds is shown by logic to be a near-certainty.

Of course, the data from which to draw the correct inferences will not always fall into your lap as it did on this
hand. Sometimes you will have to go out and look for it.

From now on there will be just the two hands on view, giving you a chance to do the work yourself.

♠ J 10 6 3
♡ Q 7 6 4   *Game all*
♢ 8 3   *Dealer West*
♣ K 10 5

W	N	E	S
—	—	—	1 ♡

♠ K
♡ K 8 5 3 2
♢ A J 10
♣ A Q J 3

W	N	E	S
—	2 ♡	—	4 ♡
All pass			

West leads the king of diamonds and you win the trick with the ace. How should you continue?

Since there is a loser in both diamonds and spades, the problem boils down to restricting the trump losers to one. There will be no difficulty about that if the trumps are 2–2, but a 3–1 break is rather more probable. In the latter case the only chance of avoiding two trump losers is to find either opponent with a singleton ace and lead through him on the first round. How can you find out who has the ace of trumps?

Well, a good way of locating honour cards in one suit is by investigating another. Here you have nothing to lose and may have a great deal to gain by playing the king of spades at trick two.

If East wins the trick you will be no further forward, since either opponent may yet have the ace of trumps. But if West produces the ace of spades you will know the whole story. He passed originally, remember, and he is marked with the king and queen of diamonds. If he has the ace of spades as well he cannot have the ace of trumps, for that would bring his point-count up to the magical number of thirteen.

You will therefore know to enter dummy as soon as you regain the lead in order to play a small trump from the table.

The next hand is rather more complex.

♠ J 9 6 2
♡ 10 5 3   *Love all*
◇ K 8 7 2   *Dealer North*
♣ J 6   W   N   E   S
                    —   —   1 ♠
♠ A Q 10 8 5   —   2 ♠   —   4 ♠
♡ A 9 2   *All pass*
◇ A 5
♣ K 8 3

West leads the eight of hearts, East puts in the knave and you win with the ace. How should you continue?

Since there are two losers in hearts it might appear at first glance that you need both the spade finesse and the ace of clubs to be right. This is wishful thinking, however. If you clear your mind and go through the proper motions you will realize that there is no way for both finesses to be right. East passed originally and is already marked with six points in hearts. The king of spades and the ace of clubs would give him thirteen.

So you have to plan the play in the certain knowledge that at least one of the key cards is badly placed. One possibility is to play for East to hold the ace of clubs and West the singleton king of spades, but that is a slender chance. It must be better to hope for East to have the king and another spade and the queen of clubs, in which case you may be able to prepare an end-play against him. Dummy does not have the entries to eliminate the diamonds completely, but a partial elimination will succeed if East has no more than three diamonds.

You should cash the ace of diamonds, lead a diamond to the king, and run the nine of spades. Then ruff a diamond and cash the ace of spades, hoping to drop the king. If all has gone well you can exit with a heart. After cashing two heart tricks East may have to choose between leading a club away from his queen or giving you a ruff and discard.

♠ K J 7 6 2
♡ 5 4
◇ J 7 5 3
♣ A 6

Game all
Dealer West

♠ A 10 9 5 4
♡ K 10
◇ A Q 6 2
♣ J 9

W	N	E	S
—	—	—	1 ♠
—	3 ♠	—	4 ♠
All pass			

West leads the king of clubs and you win with dummy's ace. Both opponents follow when you lead a trump to your ace. On the next spade West plays the queen, dummy the king, and East discards a club. How should you continue?

You have a club loser and a probable diamond loser, so the problem is to avoid the loss of two heart tricks. You may be tempted to throw West in with the club at this stage, but that would not be a logical move. West might be able to exit safely with a diamond, and you could find yourself losing a diamond trick to East and subsequently two heart tricks.

Provided that the diamonds break no worse than 3–2, however, you can make absolutely sure of your contract by taking a diamond finesse at this point. West passed originally and is marked with the queen of spades and the king and queen of clubs. He therefore cannot hold both the king of diamonds and the ace of hearts, for that would give him fourteen points. If the queen of diamonds wins you follow with the ace and then, if the king has not dropped, exit with the club. West will be compelled either to open up the hearts or give you a ruff and discard.

If the queen of diamonds loses to the king there is no need to worry, for you can be certain that the ace of hearts will be right.

♠ K 10 7 4
♡ A Q 3   *Game all*
♢ J 9 6 4   *Dealer North*
♣ 8 2

W	N	E	S
—	—		1 ♠

♠ Q J 8 6 5 3   —   3 ♠   —   4 ♠
♡ 8 5   *All pass*
♢ K 5
♣ A K 7

West leads the knave of clubs and you win with the ace. You lead a spade to the king and ace, win the club return with the king and cash the queen of spades, on which West discards a club. How do you continue?

All you know at this stage is that East, who passed originally, is marked with the ace of spades and the queen of clubs. The rest of the evidence has to be imagined. First, give East a hypothetical ace of diamonds, bringing his tally up to ten points. In that case he cannot have the king of hearts as well, so the heart finesse (and the contract) is bound to succeed. The dangerous case is where East has the king of hearts and West the ace of diamonds. Is there any way of avoiding four losers if that is the position? There is only one chance, and that is to play for East to have the queen of diamonds without the ten (giving him a plausible total of eleven points).

The correct play at this point, therefore, is to lead the five of diamonds from hand. West cannot gain by going up with the ace in order to lead a heart, and if West plays low you will put in the nine from dummy. If this draws the queen the opponents will be unable to attack the hearts before you establish a discard on the third round of diamonds.

If you got that one right you hardly need to be studying this chapter. It is certainly unusual to lead the low card from king and another, but the logic behind the play is impeccable and springs from the realization that the contract is in no danger when East has the ace of diamonds.

For once let us have a look at all four hands and see the distribution we are guarding against.

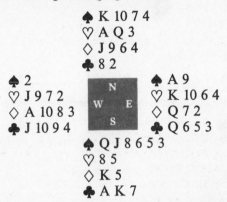

♠ K 10 7 4
♡ A Q 3
◇ J 9 6 4
♣ 8 2

♠ 2
♡ J 9 7 2
◇ A 10 8 3
♣ J 10 9 4

♠ A 9
♡ K 10 6 4
◇ Q 7 2
♣ Q 6 5 3

♠ Q J 8 6 5 3
♡ 8 5
◇ K 5
♣ A K 7

In a pairs game, of course, you could not afford the luxury of this safety play. The sensible thing to do would be to play with the field, tackling both red suits normally and hoping to make an overtrick.

To revert to basic syllogical argument for a moment, it should be pointed out that there are hazards for the unwary in hypothetical reasoning. It is all too easy to construct a false syllogism such as the following:

Major premiss—If West has thirteen high-card points he will open the bidding.
Minor premiss—He opens the bidding.
Conclusion —Therefore he has thirteen high-card points.

All bridge players know the conclusion to be false. Even if pre-emptive and psychic bids are discounted, we know that in the normal course of events players frequently open the bidding with less than thirteen points.

What went wrong with the syllogism? Well, we have read into the major premiss something that is not there. Order is

of the utmost importance in logic. From the truth of the
antecedent we can infer the truth of the consequent, but we
cannot validly reverse the order. The major premiss did not
affirm: 'If West opens the bidding he will have thirteen high-
card points', and if it had done it would have been a false
premiss.

Nevertheless, although an opening bid at the one-level does
not guarantee thirteen high-card points, the opener will not
normally be too far short of that number. A minimum of
nine points is a good working yardstick, and you should not
go wrong in the play of the following hand.

♠ 6 4
♡ K J 7 2   *N–S game*
◇ A J 8 4   *Dealer West*
♣ A Q 3   W   N   E   S
                1 ♠   Dbl   3 ♠   4 ♠
♠ A   —   5 ◇   —   5 ♡
♡ Q 9 6 5 4   —   6 ♡   *All pass*
◇ K 2
♣ K J 9 5 2

West leads the king of spades to your ace. What do you
play at trick two?

The lead of a low trump towards dummy is the standard
play to cater for all four trumps in the East hand. But that
distribution is logically impossible here. This is a one-horse
race. West is marked with the ace of hearts for his opening
bid, and only he can have four trumps.

The correct card to play at trick two is therefore the queen
of hearts, which guards against this possibility. If West wins
and East shows out, you have the entries in hand to finesse
twice against the eight and ten of hearts and bring home the
slam.

Seven is another magic number in the configurations of the

Milton Work point-count. It is the number of high-card points with which a player can be relied on to respond to his partner's opening bid. He may, of course, respond with six, five, or even fewer points, but he will not fail to respond with seven.

Thus we can construct a further series of hypothetical syllogisms starting with the major premiss: 'If West had held seven high-card points he would have responded to his partner's opening bid.' As before, the inferences that arise can be illuminating.

♠ A 6			
♡ A J 9 3		*Game all*	
◇ K J 8 5 3		*Dealer East*	
♣ 8 4	*W*	*N*	*E*	*S*

W	N	E	S
		1 ♠	—

♠ K 5 4	—	Dbl	—	3 ♡
♡ Q 10 8 7 4 2	—	4 ♡	*All pass*	
◇ 7			
♣ K 6 3			

West leads the nine of spades against your contract of four hearts. How do you plan the play?

There is a sure loser in diamonds and a possible loser in hearts, but the contract is in no danger unless the ace of clubs is badly placed. If West has the ace of clubs, however, he cannot have the king of hearts as well. With seven high-card points he would not have passed his partner's opening bid.

It would be unwise to win the first trick in hand and stake everything on an immediate trump finesse. The trumps can wait until you have discovered more about the minor suits. You should win the first trick with the ace of spades and lead a club from the table at trick two.

If East produces the ace of clubs, or if your king wins the trick, you can subsequently check the position of the ace of diamonds. When East proves to have that ace as well you can try for an overtrick by taking the trump finesse.

If West captures your king of clubs with the ace, however, you will know that the trump finesse cannot succeed. Your only chance of making the contract will be to play the ace of hearts on the first round, hoping to drop the singleton king from the East hand.

On the next example it would be easy to go wrong, but an inference from the play together with a count of points should keep you on the right track.

♠ A 6 5
♡ 9 4 2　　　　　　　　　*Game all*
◇ A 8 4　　　　　　　　*Dealer West*
♣ K 9 8 5

W	N	E	S
1 ♡	—	—	1 ♠
—	3 ♠	All pass	

♠ K J 8 4 2
♡ J 7
◇ K J 6
♣ 10 7 3

West leads the ten of diamonds, and when dummy goes down you see that your partner's double raise was on the optimistic side. Prospects are no better than fair. The ace of clubs is likely to be right, but with two losers in both hearts and clubs you will need to avoid a trump loser in order to make the contract.

You play a low diamond from dummy, East produces the queen and you win with the king. Both opponents follow with small cards when you lead a spade to the ace, and East plays the ten on the second round. Which card do you play from hand?

The normal percentage play is to finesse the knave, and this must be the right thing to do if East's ten is a true card. But there is something about the early play that may strike you as a little odd. Why should West lead from a ten-high diamond holding instead of cashing a top heart to have a look at dummy? The answer almost certainly is that he does not have the king of hearts.

Suddenly your problem is resolved. If East has the king of hearts along with his queen of diamonds, he cannot, in view of his pass of the opening bid, have the queen of spades as well. The only hope, therefore, is to put up the king of spades and find a doubleton queen in the West hand.

We shall meet further examples of this sort of inference from the play of the cards in a later chapter.

2. Out for the Count

To the bridge player the number thirteen is significant in more ways than one. We have already seen its importance in relation to the Milton Work point-count, and we are now going to study the part it has to play in the assessment of distribution. Thirteen is not only the number of cards in each suit of the pack, but also the number of cards dealt to each player at the table. These twin facts provide the entire basis for the science of 'counting the hand', by which is meant working out the distribution of all four suits in the unseen hands.

The ability to count the hand used to be considered the hallmark of the master player, but such is the improvement in the general standard of play that this is no longer the case. It may be an exaggeration to say that everyone is doing it, but many keen players have discovered that it is not, after all, so difficult to add up to, or subtract from, thirteen, and that the results can be highly gratifying.

Counting is an essential preliminary to the proper execution of advanced plays such as coups, eliminations and squeezes. An accurate count can often prove its worth in simpler situations as well, for example by turning a finesse into a certainty rather than a gamble. Counting is, in fact, the one ingredient common to all successful plays. It has rightly been described as the high road to expert country.

If we break it down into its simplest terms, counting can be seen as yet another example of the application of logic at the bridge table. When a defender shows out on the second round of spades, for instance, we can set down the argument in the form of a syllogism.

Major premiss—There are thirteen spades in the pack.
Minor premiss—North and South have three spades each and East has one.
Conclusion —Therefore West has six.

That conclusion by itself may be of limited value, but when the play of the hand is advanced by a few more tricks it may be possible to complete the chain of logic with a final syllogism.

Major premiss—West was dealt thirteen cards.
Minor premiss—He is known to have precisely six spades, two hearts and one diamond.
Conclusion —Therefore he has four clubs.

At this point you have a complete blueprint of the enemy distribution, and the knowledge that West has four clubs may enable you to make certain of your contract.

There is nothing difficult about the arithmetic, but it requires careful observation and a trained memory to collect and store the data for the minor premiss. You must not fail to notice East's discard on the second round of spades, for instance, and you must make a mental note of the fact that West followed suit twice in hearts and once in diamonds before showing out. It is easy enough to miscount the whole hand if an early discard is missed. Keeping track demands an effort of concentration that many players find hard to sustain. Nevertheless, the effort is well worth making. One of the few certainties in bridge is that those who are not prepared to make this effort will not become big winners.

A perfect count of the hand will be achieved only when the defenders have shown out in three suits. This will not normally happen until a late stage in the play, and we shall often need to formulate a plan of attack before obtaining a complete count. Then we may have to rely on an inferential count, drawing inferences from the bidding, the opening lead and the subsequent play to build up a picture of the enemy hands. When a player makes a vulnerable overcall, for instance, we can normally rely on him for five cards in his suit. When he pre-empts at the three-level we can place him with six or seven cards according to the quality of the suit and the vulnerability. When a defender leads a fourth-highest card he gives valuable information about the distribution of the suit.

The picture thus obtained, while not infallible, will often be sufficiently accurate to guide us to the best line of play. When still more information is required we may have to go out and search for it, planning the play of the hand so as to discover as much as possible about the distribution before committing ourselves in the critical suit. We may be able to discover all we need to know about one suit by investigating the distribution of another.

Inevitably there will be occasions when we lack the time for any investigation, being compelled for one reason or another to make an immediate decision about the distribution of the trump suit. Then the only count available will be a hypothetical one, which can be of considerable value owing to the interdependence of suit distributions. When the success of the contract depends on finding a particular distribution in one suit, we should assume that distribution to exist and build up our picture of the holdings in the other suits to conform with the favourable assumption. The exercise may provide a clue to the lie of the trump suit.

Let us look at a straightforward counting situation.

♠ A K J 4
♡ 7 4
◇ 7 3 2   *N–S game*
♣ K Q 6 3   *Dealer North*

	W	N	E	S
		1 ♣	3 ♡	3 NT

♠ 10 5 3   *All pass*
♡ A 10 3
◇ K Q 5
♣ A 9 5 4

West leads the eight of hearts and East plays the knave.
When you allow this to hold the trick East continues with the
king of hearts, and West discards a diamond on your ace.
You probe the diamond distribution by leading the king. West
takes his ace and returns the knave of diamonds, which you
allow to win. Your queen of diamonds scores on the third
round, with East following suit three times.

You then lead a club to the queen and cash the ace of
spades. Both defenders follow suit with low cards, but when
you return a club to your ace East discards a heart. How
should you continue?

You have seen all the evidence, but have you taken the
trouble to count the hand? East has shown up with seven
hearts, three diamonds, one club and one spade, and you
know his thirteenth card to be a spade. The spade finesse is
most likely to be right, but you can never make your contract
if it is. With only three tricks in clubs and one in each of the
red suits, you need four tricks from spades to bring your
total up to nine. And you cannot score four tricks by finessing
since the suit is known to be breaking 4–2.

There is only one holding that will allow you to score four
tricks in spades. You must lead your small spade to the king
in the hope of dropping the doubleton queen.

Now try your hand at a simple inferential count.

♠ 7 6 2
♡ Q 6 5 3   *Game all*
◇ 10 8 3   *Dealer South*
♣ A Q 5   S   W   N   E
          1 ♡   1 ♠   2 ♡   —
♠ K 8 4   4 ♡   *All pass*
♡ A K J 4 2
◇ A K 5
♣ 8 2

West leads the ten of hearts, East plays the seven and you win in hand with the knave. On the ace and king of trumps East discards the four of clubs and the two of diamonds. You take a successful club finesse, cash the ace of clubs and ruff the small club, West following with the three, the nine and the king. When you cash the ace and king of diamonds West plays the six and the nine, East the four and the seven. How should you continue?

If you are tempted to exit with the third diamond in the hope that West will have to win, you have not been doing your chores. West has already shown up with three trumps and three clubs, and his vulnerable overcall surely indicates a holding of five spades. That leaves room in his hand for only two diamonds and you have seen them both.

To exit with the diamond will work only when West has A Q J 10 9 in spades, in which case the lead of a small spade will do as well. On the one reasonable assumption that West will have the ace of spades, however, you can make certain of your contract by exiting with the king of spades.

This lead will have a deadly effect on the enemy communications. Depending on who wins the second round of spades, the defenders will be able to score either three spade tricks or two spades and a diamond, but will then have to concede a ruff and discard.

♠ K 8 3
♡ 10 5   *Match-point pairs*
◇ Q J 6 4 3   *Love all*
♣ J 6 2   *Dealer South*

	S	W	N	E
♠ 10 9 4	1 ♡	—	1 NT	2 ◇
♡ A K Q J 4	2 ♡	All pass		
◇ 5				
♣ A Q 9 3				

West leads the king of diamonds and switches to the queen of spades, which you cover with the king. East takes his ace and returns the ten of diamonds. Having no useful discard to make, you ruff high while West discards the four of clubs. After drawing trumps, which prove to be 3–3, you lead the ten of spades to West's knave. He returns a spade to your nine and East follows suit. How should you continue?

The contract is safe enough, since you have five trump tricks, one spade and at least two clubs, but you are naturally anxious to make an overtrick. What do you know about the distribution? East has shown up with six diamonds and three cards in both hearts and spades. You cannot be certain who has the last spade, but you know that East has no more than one club. The odds are against this being the king, so it must be right to lead a small club towards the knave. If East shows out on this trick, it means that West has nothing left but clubs and you can throw him in by returning a club to your nine. If East plays a small club under the knave, he can have nothing left but diamonds and you can end-play him by leading the queen of diamonds and discarding a club from your hand.

Note that you cannot afford to guard against a singleton king by cashing the ace of clubs on the first round. West might then block the clubs by playing the king on the next round and hold you to eight tricks by forcing you with the last spade.

```
  ♠ K 9 8 7
  ♡ K Q 9 3              Match-point pairs
  ◇ 8 6 4 3                 N–S game
  ♣ A                     Dealer South
                      S       W     N       E
  ♠ A Q J 5          2 NT     —    3 ♣     5 ♣
  ♡ A 7 5            Dbl      —    6 ♣     —
  ◇ A Q 5            6 ♠    All pass
  ♣ K 10 9
```

West leads the queen of clubs, and as dummy goes down it
occurs to you that East must be a bit of a joker. Both opponents follow suit when you lead a spade to the knave at trick
two. On the ten of clubs West discards the seven of diamonds.
You ruff in dummy and draw three more rounds of trumps,
East discarding three clubs and dummy a diamond. West
throws the nine of diamonds on the king of clubs, and you
let go another diamond from the table. You continue with
the ace of hearts and a heart to the king, East playing the ten
on the second round. What now?

East is marked with eight clubs, one spade, two hearts and
two more red cards. Although you have only eleven top
tricks at this point, the contract must be perfectly safe. Suppose you cash the queen of hearts and East shows out. That
is nothing to worry about for you can throw West in with
the fourth heart to lead up to your diamonds. If West shows
out on the third heart East must be void in diamonds, and
you simply duck a diamond to West to achieve the throw-in.
And if the hearts break 3–3 you will make an overtrick when
East's singleton diamond is the king.

Are you satisfied with this line of play or do you suspect a
flaw in the analysis? In fact the plan is not ambitious enough,
for if you cash the queen of hearts at this point you are giving
up the chance of a safe overtrick when the hearts are with
West. The logical play is a diamond from the table.

If East shows out you will have to settle for twelve tricks

by ducking the trick to West. If East follows, however, you can afford to finesse the queen. If this wins, it means that the diamonds are 2–2, in which case the five of diamonds will provide the thirteenth trick. If the diamond finesse loses there is still no need to worry, for either the diamonds or the hearts must break to give you a twelfth trick.

These hypothetical count situations can be confusing because the reasoning involved allows for so many alternatives. Reducing the argument to the simplest terms, the diamond play is safe because (a) if East is void you can duck to West, (b) if East has a singleton the hearts must be 3–3, and (c) if East has a doubleton the five of diamonds becomes a trick.

The full hand:

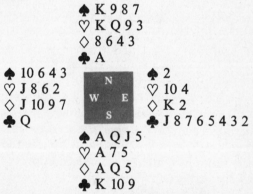

                ♠ K 9 8 7
                ♡ K Q 9 3
                ◇ 8 6 4 3
                ♣ A
  ♠ 10 6 4 3   ♠ 2
  ♡ J 8 6 2   ♡ 10 4
  ◇ J 10 9 7   ◇ K 2
  ♣ Q   ♣ J 8 7 6 5 4 3 2
                ♠ A Q J 5
                ♡ A 7 5
                ◇ A Q 5
                ♣ K 10 9

This fascinating hand comes from the first World Pairs Championship in Cannes in 1962. It was reported in *Bridge Magazine* by the late M. Harrison Gray.

On the next few hands it will not be enough to sit back and wait for information about the enemy distribution to come to you. A conscious effort to gather such information is what is required.

♠ A 8 2
♡ A J 5
◇ K 10 7 4   *Love all*
♣ 6 5 2   *Dealer South*
        S   *N*
♠ Q 7 4   1 NT 3 NT
♡ 8 6 3
◇ A Q 3
♣ K Q J 4

West leads the knave of spades, and when you play low from dummy East produces the king. He returns the ten of clubs and West captures your king with the ace. West tries a third suit (a little late) when he switches to the ten of hearts. Dummy's knave is captured by the queen, and East returns the nine of clubs to your queen. West discards a spade on the second round of clubs, and when you cash the queen of spades East discards a club. What next?

With only eight top tricks you must hope for the diamond suit to provide the ninth. What do you know about the hand so far? Simply that West started with six spades and a club, East with five clubs and a spade. Both have followed to one round of hearts, but the distribution of the red suits is still obscure. More information is needed. In order to determine how to play the diamonds you must first probe the distribution of the heart suit. The way to do that is to concede a fourth trick to the defence by ducking a heart at this point. You will win the return and cash the ace of hearts to unlock the secret of the diamonds.

If West proves to have no more than two hearts, you will know that he has four diamonds and will make the contract by taking a third-round finesse against the knave. If West follows to a third round of hearts, he can have no more than three diamonds. In that case the diamonds may be 3–3, but even if they are not the next play of the ace of spades will squeeze East in the minor suits.

♠ A 5
♡ A K 4
◇ Q J 5 3   *N–S game*
♣ K 7 3 2   *Dealer South*

	S	W	N	E
♠ K J	1 NT	3 ♠	6 NT	*All pass*

♡ J 7 3
◇ A 10 9 6
♣ A Q 9 5

West leads the ten of spades and you can count twelve
tricks if both minor suits behave well. You win in dummy
with the ace and run the queen of diamonds, which holds the
trick. You continue with a diamond to your nine, and your
ace fells the king on the third round, West discarding a spade.
Both opponents follow with small cards when you lead a
heart to the ace. What is the next move?

I hope you are not tempted to test the clubs at this point.
True, if East proves to have a club stopper you can cash the
king of spades and throw him in with the club to lead away
from his queen of hearts. But there is no guarantee that he
has the queen of hearts.

There is no need for such a gamble, for the contract is cold
on the assumption that West has at least seven spades. He has
already shown up with three red cards and therefore can have
no more than three clubs. You need to know the precise
number of clubs he holds, and you can find out by testing the
heart distribution. The correct move at this point is to lead
the four of hearts from the table.

After winning the spade return you will lead a third heart
to the king. If West shows out on the second or third round
of hearts you will know that the clubs are breaking 3–2. If
West follows to three rounds of hearts, on the other hand, he
will be marked with one club at most. You will therefore
cash the king of clubs and lead another club for a deep finesse
of the nine. It will not help East to split his honours, for you

can return to dummy with the knave of diamonds and repeat the club finesse.

```
♠ 7 6
♡ J 10 9 3
◇ A 8 6 5                Game all
♣ A J 9                  Dealer West
                    W       N       E       S
♠ J 8 2             1 ♠     —       —       2 ♡
♡ A K Q 6 4         2 ♠     4 ♡     All pass
◇ 9 3
♣ Q 7 2
```

West attacks with the top spades, and East discards a club when you ruff the third round with the knave of hearts. How should you continue?

Clearly you need to find a favourable club position, either the king singleton or doubleton or both the king and the ten with West. In order to find out which holding to play for you must first investigate the distribution of the other suits. The correct move at this point is to play the ace and another diamond.

Let us suppose that East wins and returns a trump to which West follows. You win in dummy with the nine, ruff a diamond high while both opponents follow, and lead a trump to the ten on which West discards a spade.

A ruff of the last diamond will complete the picture. If West shows out it will be clear that he has three clubs. You will therefore need to take a deep finesse of the nine of clubs. If this wins you will return to hand with the last trump and take a further club finesse.

If West follows to the fourth diamond, however, he is marked with only two clubs. You will therefore draw the last trump, finesse the knave of clubs and continue with the ace.

Note that you will not be able to obtain a complete count if you play a round of trumps at trick four.

♠ K 5
♡ J 7 6 3
◇ A J 8 6 2   *Game all*
♣ 9 3   *Dealer South*

	S	W	N	E
♠ A Q J 10 9 8	1 ♠	—	2 ◇	2 ♡
♡ 4	4 ♠	All pass		
◇ K 3				
♣ A 10 7 2				

West wins the first trick with the queen of hearts and, annoyingly, switches to a trump. You win in hand and lead the two of clubs, but East wins with the king and returns a second trump to dummy's king. West follows suit with the two when you ruff a heart, but he discards a diamond on the third round of trumps. How should you continue?

It seems reasonable to place East with six hearts for his vulnerable overcall, and he has followed to three trumps and one club. You need to know more about the minor suit distribution, and the way to find out is by ducking a second round of clubs at this point. The lead of a small club is likely to serve the further purpose of rectifying the count for a squeeze against West.

You will win any return in hand and cash the ace of clubs to bring the picture into focus. If East follows to the third club he can have at most a singleton diamond, and you can make the contract either by taking the marked finesse or by playing off the trumps to squeeze West. If East shows out on the third round of clubs he is marked with two diamonds. Now a finesse in diamonds is both dangerous and unnecessary. You can avoid all risk by cashing your remaining trumps. This will force West to come down to two diamonds in order to retain his club stopper, and the queen of diamonds is bound to fall under the ace, no matter who holds it.

A pre-emptive bid by an opponent will often simplify your

task, helping you to obtain a quick and accurate count of the hand.

	W	N	E	S
♠ A Q		*N–S game*		
♡ A K Q 7		*Dealer East*		
◇ 6 4			3 ◇	—
♣ A K J 10 7				
♠ K 10 9 5 2	—	Dbl	—	3 ♠
♡ J 10 8 6	—	4 ♣	—	4 ♡
◇ K 7	—	5 ♡	—	6 ♡
♣ 5 4	*All pass*			

West leads the knave of diamonds to his partner's ace. East returns the queen of diamonds and West follows with the two. Both opponents follow to the ace and king of trumps, and East discards a diamond when you lead the seven of trumps to your ten. How should you continue?

East is marked with seven diamonds and two trumps. That leaves him with four cards in the black suits, and you can be sure that he will not be void in clubs since he did not double for the lead. The slam must be cold if you time your sequence of plays correctly. Can you see the sure way of making it?

You should start probing the enemy distribution by cashing the ace and king of clubs. If East shows out on the second round there is no further problem since the spades must be 3–3. If East follows to two rounds of clubs you continue by cashing the ace of spades. In the unlikely event of East showing out he is marked with four clubs, so you can run the knave of clubs with confidence.

If East follows to the ace of spades you continue with the queen. If East shows out this time, the clubs must be 3–3 and a simple ruff will establish the suit.

Finally, if East follows to the queen of spades it must be with his last black card, so you can safely overtake with the king and run the ten of spades to bring home the slam.

♠ 8 4 2
♡ K 8 2   *N–S game*
♢ A J 10 7   *Dealer South*
♣ Q 8 2   S   W   N   E
                        1 ♡   —   2 ♢   3 ♣
♠ A K   3 ♢   —   3 ♡   —
♡ A J 7 6 5   4 ♡   *All pass*
♢ Q 6 4 2
♣ 10 7

West leads the four of clubs, you play low from dummy, and
East wins with the knave. He continues with the king of
clubs, on which West discards the three of spades. When you
ruff the next lead of the ace of clubs with the five of hearts,
West over-ruffs with the nine and returns the ten of spades to
the knave and king. You draw the remaining trumps with the
king and ace, East playing the ten and the queen. How
should you continue?

Since you have already lost three tricks you need the
diamond finesse to be right, and dummy's pips are such that
you can avoid a loser even when West has four cards in the
suit. But if your lead of the queen of diamonds is covered by
the king and ace and East follows with a low card, you will
not know what to do after returning to hand with the ace of
spades. East's distribution could be either 2–2–2–7 or
3–2–1–7.

In order to obtain an accurate blueprint of the distribution
you must cash the ace of spades before leading the queen of
diamonds. When the queen is covered by the king, you win
with the ace and return to hand with a spade ruff. If East
follows to the third round of spades you will know that it is
safe to take a deep finesse on the second round of diamonds.

West will be unable to save the situation by playing the
eight or nine on the second round of diamonds since you still
have a trump entry to hand.

```
♠ A Q 10 7 3
♡ 5                    Game all
♢ A 8 7 4 2            Dealer South
♣ Q 5                  S        N
                       1 ♡      1 ♠
♠ 6                    2 ♢      4 ♢
♡ A K 7 6 2            4 NT     5 ♡
♢ K Q J 5              6 ♢      —
♣ K J 2
```

West leads the ace and another club against your diamond
slam. You win the second club with the king and cash the
king and queen of diamonds, and the hand becomes a little
awkward when East discards a spade on the second round.
You cash the knave of clubs, throwing a spade from dummy,
and East discards another spade. What now?

Holding nine cards in the minor suits, West can have only
four in the majors. You cannot afford to draw the outstanding trump at this stage, but you must guard against an over-
ruff by West. You could cope with the case where West has
two cards in each major by leading a spade to the ace and
ruffing a spade with your small trump. You could then cash
the top hearts and make the rest of the tricks on a cross-ruff.

This plan will fail if West has a singleton spade, however,
and there must be a safer alternative. In fact you can succeed
against all distributions except a void heart in the West hand
by starting with the ace and king of hearts. If West discards
on the second heart, lead a spade to the ace and cross-ruff the
remainder. If he ruffs the second heart you can over-ruff and
establish the spades by ruffing twice in hand.

If West follows twice in hearts, ruff a third heart in
dummy. If West discards this time you can return to the
knave of diamonds, squeezing East in the process. He must
weaken one of his major suits, and you will be able to ruff
out the suit in which he discards. Finally, if West follows to

three rounds of hearts you can return to the knave of diamonds and ruff another heart to establish the suit.

♠ 7 5 4
♡ A K 6 5   *Game all*
♢ 10 4 2   *Dealer South*
♣ 8 7 2

S	W	N	E
1 ♣	—	1 ♡	2 ♢

♠ A K 6   3 ♢   —   4 ♣   —
♡ 10 4   5 ♣   *All pass*
♢ J 5
♣ A K Q 10 6 5

West leads the nine of diamonds to his partner's queen. East cashes the king of diamonds and continues with the ace, and you ruff with the ace of clubs while West discards a spade. When you play the king of clubs West follows suit with the three and East with the four. How should you continue?

You know little about the enemy distribution except that East started with six diamonds and West with two. The odds must be heavily against East having three trumps, but if you project your thoughts into the future and do your homework you may realize that the contract can never be made if the trumps break 2–2.

The point is that you have no more than ten top tricks even if you manage to avoid a trump loser. The eleventh trick will have to come from a squeeze in spades and hearts, and that will be possible only when West has five cards in each major. You must play him for this hypothetical hand, and you have already seen the two diamonds and one club that make up his full complement of thirteen cards.

To give yourself a chance of making the contract, therefore, you should enter dummy in hearts and return a club for a finesse of the ten.

♠ A 3
♡ K Q 7 4
◇ Q 6 4 2   *Love all*
♣ J 10 9   *Dealer South*

	S	N
♠ 7 2	1 NT	2 ♣
♡ A J 9 3	2 ♡	4 ♡
◇ K 10 5		
♣ A 7 6 4		

West leads the knave of spades which you allow to hold
the trick. He continues with the ten of spades and East plays
the queen under dummy's ace. Both defenders follow suit
with small cards when you lead the four of hearts to your ace,
but West discards a spade when you return the three of hearts
to the queen. Your next move is to run the knave of clubs.
West produces the queen and returns the three of clubs to
dummy's ten. On the next round East covers the nine of clubs
with the king, and you win with the ace as West discards a
further spade. What now?

It is time to review the situation and do a little counting.
East has shown up with four cards in both hearts and clubs,
and from the fall of the queen of spades he appears to have
three spades. That leaves room for only two diamonds in his
hand, and you must therefore abandon any idea of finessing
the ten of diamonds. The two diamond tricks that you need
can be made only if East's doubleton includes the ace.

The diamond lead has to come from dummy, so you must
ruff your losing club first. But there is a hidden trap ahead.
If you ruff the club with the seven of trumps and lead a
diamond, East will defeat you by rising with the ace and
returning a diamond, or by winning the second diamond and
exiting with a trump. In either case you will have no way
back to hand to draw the last trump, and East will score a
diamond ruff for a fourth defensive trick.

You must therefore unblock the trumps by ruffing the

losing club with the king of hearts. Then a small diamond from the table will leave East without resource. If he plays the ace and returns a diamond, you can win with the queen and take a trump finesse. If he plays the ace and returns a spade, you can discard your king of diamonds, ruff in dummy and cash the queen of diamonds to achieve a trump coup. Nor does it help East to play low on the first diamond, for you can win with the king and duck the next round to his ace.

The full hand:

```
                    ♠ A 3
                    ♡ K Q 7 4
                    ◇ Q 6 4 2
                    ♣ J 10 9
  ♠ J 10 9 8 6 5                    ♠ K Q 4
  ♡ 5              N                ♡ 10 8 6 2
  ◇ J 8 7 3    W       E            ◇ A 9
  ♣ Q 3            S                ♣ K 8 5 2
                    ♠ 7 2
                    ♡ A J 9 3
                    ◇ K 10 5
                    ♣ A 7 6 4
```

Clearly the defence could have done better. The game can be defeated if West switches to diamonds at trick two. South cannot come to ten tricks without a club ruff, and when West regains the lead with the queen of clubs he can give his partner a diamond ruff. This defence is perhaps easier to see from the other side of the table, and East might have overtaken the knave of spades at trick one in order to play the ace and another diamond.

After the spade continuation at trick two West can still defeat the contract by switching to a diamond when in with the queen of clubs. If East plays ace and another diamond and covers the second club, South is unable to negotiate his club ruff.

3. Echoes from the Bidding

Several hands in the first two chapters give an indication of the way in which the expert relies on inferences from the bidding to help him place the high cards and count the hand. We are now going to examine this aspect of the game in greater detail.

Bidding inferences are not infallible, since it is rare for two players to bid a hand in exactly the same way. What is accepted by one player as a normal bid may strike another as sheer madness. This is clearly seen in the bidding forums conducted by bridge magazines, where many problems attract half a dozen different answers from the panel of experts. But there are certain basic inferences that can be drawn with very little danger.

When a player makes a bid that promises specific length or strength, it is normally safe to assume that he has that length or strength. He is more likely to be concerned with giving his partner honest information than with trying to pull the wool over your eyes. When an opponent opens with a bid of one no trump, for instance, it is safe to play him for a balanced hand within the prescribed point range. When he opens with a three-bid he will normally have seven cards in his suit. And when he bids and rebids his suit in a competitive auction he is unlikely to have less than six cards.

As the play progresses you should keep an ear open for echoes, referring constantly back to the bidding to make sure that your plan of campaign is in accordance with the known facts. Do not overlook the negative inferences that arise when an opponent fails to bid or fails to double.

See if you can pluck a winning inference from the silence of the defenders in this example.

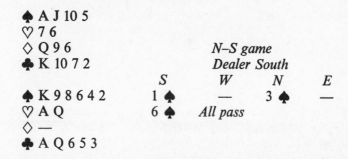

♠ A J 10 5
♡ 7 6
◇ Q 9 6   *N–S game*
♣ K 10 7 2   *Dealer South*

	S	W	N	E
♠ K 9 8 6 4 2	1 ♠	—	3 ♠	—
♡ A Q	6 ♠	*All pass*		
◇ —				
♣ A Q 6 5 3				

West leads the ace of diamonds, and when dummy goes down you are inclined to wish that you were in seven. However, your task is to make twelve tricks in safety. East encourages with the knave of diamonds and you ruff the first trick. How should you continue?

The problem is to find the best way of tackling the trumps. You can afford a trump loser provided that you do not also lose a club trick. The position of the king of hearts is irrelevant on this deal, for the second heart in dummy can be discarded on the long club.

Once you reach the conclusion that the slam is in danger only when East has a club stopper, you have an indication of the right way to play the trumps. If West is void in clubs he can hardly be void in spades as well. That would give him thirteen cards in the red suits, on which he would surely have made a first-round overcall.

You should therefore play the king of spades at trick two. If it transpires that you have to lose a trump to East, you can be sure that there will be no club loser to threaten the safety of the slam.

♠ A 5
♡ K 6 3
♢ A 10 7 6 2   *Game all*
♣ K 8 4   *Dealer South*

	S	W	N	E
♠ K Q J 10 8 6 3	1 ♠	—	2 ♢	—
♡ Q 7	4 ♠	—	6 ♠	*All pass*
♢ Q J 5				
♣ A				

The opening lead of the queen of clubs takes out your ace. How do you plan the play?

This is a reasonable slam which will always make when the diamond finesse is right. However, there are additional chances because of the interesting position in the heart suit. If you can sneak past the ace of hearts you will be home and dry, for your second heart will be discarded on the king of clubs. Nor will it help the defender to beat air with the ace of hearts, for that will give you two discards for the losing diamonds.

It is possible to play either defender for the ace of hearts. If you decide that West has it, you must lead the seven of hearts at trick two, before dummy's spade entry is spent. If West goes up with the ace of hearts and switches to a diamond, you can put up the ace, unblock the queen of hearts, cash the king and ace of spades, and take your diamond discards on the king of clubs and the king of hearts. If you decide to play East for the ace of hearts, you can cash the king and ace of spades before leading a low heart from the table. If East plays the ace he will be unable to damage you with a diamond lead, and you will be able to draw any outstanding trumps before taking your discards.

Is there any clue to the position of the ace of hearts? Nothing much can be read into the failure of either defender to make a vulnerable overcall, but what about East's final pass? With the king of diamonds *and* an ace might he not have doubled for the lead? It seems likely that he would, and you should therefore play West for the ace of hearts by leading the seven at trick two. If East produces the ace after all, the diamond finesse is most likely to succeed.

♠ K Q 7 4
♡ A Q 9 6 5 3
◇ K   *Game all*
♣ K 7   *Dealer South*

	S	W	N	E
♠ A J 9 8 6 5	1 ♠	—	4 NT	—
♡ 8	5 ♡	—	6 ♠	*All pass*
◇ A 10 8 4 3				
♣ 10				

West leads the queen of diamonds and East plays the five under dummy's king. Both opponents follow suit when you lead the four of spades to your knave, but when you test the hearts at the next trick West startles you by discarding the five of clubs. You win with the ace and hastily draw the last trump by leading the king of spades to your ace, West throwing the seven of diamonds. On the ace of diamonds you throw a heart from the table, and East also discards a heart. How should you continue?

The bad breaks in both red suits give you a complete count of the hand but you are left with only eleven sure tricks. The king of clubs may provide the twelfth trick, however. West is marked with six clubs to East's four, so at first glance the ace of clubs seems likely to be in the West hand. But the bidding tells a different story. With six diamonds headed by the queen and knave and six clubs headed by the ace, West would surely have found an overcall at the two-level. His silence in the bidding denies possession of the ace of clubs, and you must therefore abandon the idea of leading your club towards the king.

Instead you must play East for the ace of clubs. That is done easily enough by ruffing a diamond and leading a low heart from the table. When East covers this card you can discard the ten of clubs from hand, and East will have to yield the twelfth trick whether he returns a club or a heart.

```
♠ A 3
♡ A 10 4                    Love all
◇ K 8 6 3                   Dealer North
♣ 9 7 6 2        W       N      E      S
                          —     1 ♣    1 ♠
♠ K Q 10 7 5 2   2 ♣     3 ♣    —      3 ♠
♡ J 3            All pass
◇ 7 5 4
♣ A 5
```

West leads the queen of diamonds and your chances do not look very bright when dummy goes down. When you play low, however, East puts on the ace of diamonds and switches to the queen of clubs. What do you make of that?

Suddenly nine tricks appear to be within your grasp, counting six trumps, two aces and the king of diamonds. Clearly you must win this trick with the ace of clubs, for you cannot afford to allow West to lead another diamond until trumps have been drawn. Are there any special considerations that will affect your handling of the trumps?

If you refer back to the bidding you will realize that the trump position has already been charted for you. East can have no more than four clubs since his partner supported the suit, and he is marked with a singleton diamond. With a five-card heart suit he would surely have opened one heart rather than one club, and the logical conclusion is that his distribution is 4-4-1-4.

After leading a trump to the ace, therefore, you should finesse the ten on the way back to make your nine tricks.

♠ K Q 10 6 5 2
♡ 10
◇ 7 6 4
♣ 8 4 3

Match-point pairs
Game all
Dealer South

S	W	N	E
1 ♡	Dbl	1 ♠	—
2 ♣	*All pass*		

♠ 4
♡ Q J 8 5 2
◇ K 8 3
♣ A Q 9 5

West leads the two of clubs, and when dummy goes down
you wish you had passed one spade. You capture East's ten
of clubs with the queen and lead a heart, which West wins
with the king. West continues the trump attack, leading the
king to knock out your ace while East follows with the six. A
small heart brings forth the ace from West and you ruff on
the table.

Your next move is to lead the king of spades, on which
East plays the knave. West appears not to like this develop-
ment. After some thought he plays low, and you continue
with the queen of spades, East throwing a diamond and you
a small heart. This time West takes his ace and returns the
nine of spades to dummy's ten, East discarding a heart and
you a diamond. What now?

You have scored five tricks, and if the diamond ace is
right you can make your contract by leading a diamond at
this point. West has shown up with fifteen high-card points
in the other three suits and does not need to have the ace of
diamonds for his double. You know that he has precisely two
cards in diamonds, since he is marked with five spades, four
clubs and two hearts.

It is when you consider the Eastern silence that the picture
comes into focus. With five diamonds headed by the ace,
surely East would not have sold out to two clubs. You should
therefore settle quietly for one down by ruffing a spade and

leading a heart. Minus 100 should be worth a few match
points, whereas minus 200 or 300 would be a disaster.

♠ A 6 4
♡ Q 10 5   *E–W game*
◇ 9 8 5   *Dealer East*
♣ A 10 8 2   *W*   *N*   *E*   *S*

                                              1 ♠   2 ♡

♠ K 3   2 ♠   3 ♡   —   4 ♡
♡ A J 9 8 6 4 3   *All pass*
◇ Q 6 2
♣ 7

West leads the ten of diamonds to his partner's king. East
continues with the ace of diamonds on which West plays the
three. The next lead of the knave of diamonds is ruffed by
West with the two of hearts, and the ten of spades is returned.
How should you proceed?

The diamond position was a bit of a surprise, with East
proving to have five cards in the suit. Since he chose to open
one spade he must also have five spades, which leaves him
with only three cards in hearts and clubs. If he is void in
hearts there will be no way of avoiding a further loser, but
you should be able to pick up the trumps without loss when
East has either one or two cards in the suit.

The way to find out whether a trump finesse is needed or
not is to investigate the club distribution. Since East must
have at least one club it is perfectly safe to do this. You
should win the spade lead in hand with the king, lead a club
to the ace and continue with another club. If East follows to
this trick he can have no more than one trump, so you can
ruff and lay down the ace of hearts.

If East shows out on the second round of clubs you will
know that he has the guarded king of trumps. You will
therefore ruff, return to the ace of spades, and run the queen
of hearts to bring home the contract.

♠ 4
♡ A 7 6 3   *N–S game*
♦ 9 8 3 2   *Dealer South*
♣ K 9 5 2

S	W	N	E
1 ♡	2 ♠*	3 ♡	—
3 NT	—	4 ♡	*All pass*

♠ A J 6 2
♡ K Q J 5
♦ Q 10 7 4
♣ A

* * Weak jump overcall, 6–10 points*

West leads the nine of hearts, East plays the four and you win with the knave. Both opponents follow suit when you continue with the king of hearts, and after cashing the ace of clubs you enter dummy with the ace of hearts, on which East discards the four of clubs. When you run the nine of diamonds East plays the five and West the ace. West returns the ten of spades to his partner's queen. Take it from there.

There will be no problem if the diamonds are 3–2, but it is quite possible that East has all the remaining diamonds. In that case, if you ruff the second spade and lead a low diamond East will defeat you by ducking. If you lead the eight of diamonds he will take his king and return a diamond, leaving you with two losing spades. Neither will it help to discard a spade on the king of clubs before leading a diamond. East will then take his king and force you with a club.

The only way to cope with a 4–1 diamond break is to preserve your spade ruff for a later stage. Since on the bidding the spades are bound to be 6–2, you can do this by allowing the defence to win the second round of spades, discarding a club from dummy instead of ruffing. West will be unable to lead another spade without giving you a second trick in the suit. He will therefore have to lead a club, presenting you with the extra entry to dummy that you need. You can discard a spade on the king of clubs and lead a diamond, and East will be powerless to defeat the contract.

```
♠ K 5 3
♡ 9 8 7 4 3                  Game all
◇ 6                          Dealer West
♣ K J 9 3          W        N        E        S
                   1 ♠       —        —        Dbl
♠ J 8 4 2          2 ◇      2 ♡      3 ◇      3 NT
♡ A Q 5            Dbl     All pass
◇ K J 5
♣ A Q 10
```

West leads the four of diamonds and you capture East's queen with the king. Both defenders follow suit when you cash the ace of clubs. How should you continue?

Having only six top tricks, you need to develop three more for your contract. The heart suit looks the most promising source of extra tricks, but any idea of crossing to dummy and taking the heart finesse must be abandoned. East's first-round pass and West's final double both indicate that the king of hearts is likely to be in the West hand.

The bidding seems to place West with five cards in both spades and diamonds, however, in which case he can have no more than two hearts. Something might be achieved, therefore, by cashing the ace of hearts at trick three. If West plays his small card, you will be able to establish all the tricks you need by continuing with the small heart from hand.

West may have a singleton king of hearts, of course, or he may unblock with a doubleton by throwing his king under the ace. The appearance of the king need not bother you, for you can continue with a spade to the king and three more rounds of clubs, throwing the small heart from hand and watching West's discards. His hand will be easily counted, and you will know what to do after returning to hand with the queen of hearts. If West bares the ace of diamonds you will throw him in with it. After cashing two spades he will have to let you make the rest of the tricks. Otherwise you will exit in spades, and West will have to concede a trick to your knave of diamonds at the end. That will teach him to double *you*.

♠ A 9 4 2		*Love all*		
♡ A K Q 8 4		*Dealer North*		
◇ —	*W*	*N*	*E*	*S*
♣ Q 8 5 2		1 ♡	2 ♠*	3 ◇
	—	3 ♡	—	4 NT
♠ 6	—	5 ♡	—	6 ◇
♡ 9 3 2	*All pass*			
◇ A K Q 10 9 6 4				
♣ K 3				

* *Roman jump overcall, 5–5 in the black suits with about 10 points*

West leads the three of spades to dummy's ace. How do you plan the play?

Two-suited overcalls may be good for contesting the auction but they give a lot away when the other side wins the declaration. In this case you know that West is likely to have a trump trick and you count yourself lucky to have escaped a club lead. If there *is* a trump loser you will need to get both clubs away before losing the lead, which will be possible only when West has four hearts.

Suppose you ruff a spade at trick two and cash the top trumps to find East discarding on the third round. You will then be unable to cater for all the 4–1 heart breaks. If you take a deep finesse on the first round you may lose to a singleton knave or ten, while if you start with the ace you will fail when East produces a small heart. You can return to hand by ruffing a spade, but West will split his honours on the next round of hearts and you will be left with no way back to hand.

To clarify the situation, therefore, you must cash one top heart at trick two. Then ruff a spade and test the trumps, and you will know what to do if it transpires that you have a trump loser.

There is no danger of a heart ruff, for if East had been void he would surely have Lightner-doubled for the lead.

♠ Q 5 3		N–S game		
♡ 4 3		Dealer South		
◇ A K 7 5	S	W	N	E
♣ K 9 6 2	1 ♠	3 ◇*	Dbl	3 ♡
	—	—	3 ♠	—
♠ A K 7 6 2	4 ♠	All pass		
♡ Q 7				
◇ 6 4				
♣ A 8 4 3				

* Roman jump overcall, 5–5 in the red suits with about 10 points

West cashes the ace and king of hearts and switches to the ten of spades. How do you plan the play?

There are nine top tricks if the trumps break evenly, and you will need to find the tenth trick in clubs. But will that be possible? Thanks to the Roman jump overcall you already know a good deal about the distribution. West has admitted to ten cards in the red suits, and you require him to have two trumps if the contract is to have a chance. That leaves room in his hand for only one club, which is likely to complicate your task of scoring three club tricks.

There will be no real problem when West has a singleton honour. In that case, when trumps have been drawn, a club to the king followed by a small club from the table will ensure three tricks in the suit. But if West's singleton is a small card, the contract will be made only if you can remove East's exit cards, reducing him to a position where he has nothing but clubs left in his hand. Then a club to dummy's nine will end-play him.

Such a position cannot be achieved by cashing the top diamonds and running the trumps, for East will discard a club on the last trump, keeping a heart as an exit card. Does this mean that the contract cannot be made when West has a small singleton club? Not a bit of it. When pressure cannot be applied in one way it is worth while looking for another, and in this case East's exit cards can be effectively removed by forcing him to discard on diamonds.

Winning the first trump in hand, you should lead a diamond to the ace, cash the king, and play a third diamond. There is no need to worry about a possible uppercut. An uppercut from three trumps will do no harm, and if East has only two trumps the contract can never be made. Assuming East discards a heart, you will ruff, lead a trump to the queen and play the fourth diamond.

This time East will really feel the pressure. If he discards his last heart you will ruff, draw the last trump, and lead a club, putting in dummy's nine if West contributes a low card. East will have to concede the rest of the tricks on the club return. If East discards a club on the fourth diamond, you will ruff and play three rounds of clubs, leaving the last trump outstanding. Again East will have to concede the rest of the tricks whether he returns his trump or his heart.

The full hand:

```
              ♠ Q 5 3
              ♡ 4 3
              ◇ A K 7 5
              ♣ K 9 6 2
♠ 10 9                        ♠ J 8 4
♡ A K J 9 2      N            ♡ 10 8 6 5
◇ Q J 10 9 3   W   E          ◇ 8 2
♣ 5              S            ♣ Q J 10 7
              ♠ A K 7 6 2
              ♡ Q 7
              ◇ 6 4
              ♣ A 8 4 3
```

Note that East cannot escape by ruffing the fourth diamond. After over-ruffing you will be left with a trump in each hand, and a club to the nine will still produce a happy ending.

```
♠ J 7
♥ Q 5                          N–S game
♦ J 10 9 4 2                   Dealer West
♣ A Q J 5              W       N        E          S
                       1 ♠     —        2 ♦        2 ♥
♠ Q 10 4               2 ♠     3 ♥      —          4 ♥
♥ K J 10 9 7 4 3       —       —        Dbl        All pass
♦ —
♣ K 7 2
```

West leads the ace of diamonds and you ruff the first trick.
How should you continue?

At first glance there appear to be only three losers—two
spades and a trump. When you reflect on the bidding, however, you may hear the warning bells. East is marked with
the ace of hearts for his double, and to judge from West's
rebid and East's failure to support, the spades would appear
to be 6–2. If you lead a heart immediately East will hold off.
He will win the second trump and lead spades, scoring a
fourth trick for the defence with a spade ruff.

The way to overcome this threat is by leading spades yourself, aiming to cut communications while the queen of
trumps remains in dummy to protect against an over-ruff. It
will do the defenders no good to counter by ducking a round
of trumps. You will win in hand and continue with a second
spade, and when East gets in with the ace of hearts he will
have no spade left to lead.

The most awkward defence will be for East to win the first
spade and continue with a small diamond. After ruffing, you
will feel some anxiety about being forced if East started with
all four trumps. The danger is more apparent than real,
however, for at this stage you can clarify the position by
leading the nine of trumps. Whether he started with three
trumps or four, East must duck to create any problem. You
continue with a second spade to West, who can trouble you
only by leading another diamond, presumably his second

honour card (you know, of course, that West must have a second honour in diamonds if East has one of the top spades). After accepting the force you will not be able to afford to draw trumps if East started with four trumps. Instead you can lead a club to the knave and run the knave of diamonds, discarding a club if East refuses to cover. Then a club to your king followed by a ruff of the third spade with the queen of hearts will bring your total up to ten tricks.

You will still make the contract if the diamonds prove to be 4–4, for you will then be able to score three club tricks.

The full hand:

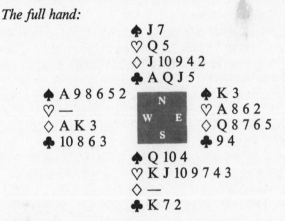

```
                    ♠ J 7
                    ♡ Q 5
                    ◇ J 10 9 4 2
                    ♣ A Q J 5
  ♠ A 9 8 6 5 2                    ♠ K 3
  ♡ —                  N           ♡ A 8 6 2
  ◇ A K 3          W     E         ◇ Q 8 7 6 5
  ♣ 10 8 6 3          S           ♣ 9 4
                    ♠ Q 10 4
                    ♡ K J 10 9 7 4 3
                    ◇ —
                    ♣ K 7 2
```

On this lie of the cards the only lead to defeat the contract is the unlikely one of a club.

4. Pointers from the Play

When the bidding does not help, you may have to rely on inferences from the fall of the cards to guide you to the winning line of play. There is a gradual accumulation of knowledge as the play of the hand progresses. Not only do the defenders yield information about the distribution whenever they show out, but the very nature and direction of their attack provides additional clues to their holdings.

If the defenders play a forcing game, for instance, you should not be surprised to find the trumps breaking unevenly. When the defenders lead trumps you are likely to discover that your side suit is well held.

The quality of the opposition is a factor to be considered, for this may affect the validity of any inferences that you draw. Weak players defend erratically because they are fumbling in the dark. Since they themselves seldom know what they are about, it is hard to interpret their moves with any degree of accuracy.

You are on much safer ground when the opponents are experienced players. Their actions will be dictated by reason and will therefore be open to logical interpretation. When a capable player adopts an unusual line of defence, or fails to adopt an obvious line, you should at once be on the alert. In order to work out what he is trying to do to you, you will have to creep inside his head and examine his thought-processes. Often it will be possible to conclude that he could not have defended in that way unless he held (or did not hold) a particular card.

Of course a good opponent will be probing your thoughts while you are examining his, and at the highest level the game can develop into one of bluff and counter-bluff. But as a general rule you can expect honest cards from the defenders, for their need to feed each other accurate information is greater than their desire to lead you astray.

The strongest inferences are those that are valid irrespective of the class of the opposition. Here is a simple example.

```
♠ J 9 4
♡ A Q 10
♢ K 6                    Game all
♣ K J 8 7 3             Dealer West
                    W        N       E       S
♠ A Q 10 7 6 5      1 ◇      Dbl     1 ♡     4 ♠
♡ K 3               All pass
♢ 8 5 4 2
♣ 6
```

West leads the ace of diamonds on which his partner plays the nine. When the three of diamonds is continued at trick two, East ruffs with the two of spades and returns a club. West wins with the ace and switches to the knave of hearts, which you win in dummy with the queen. What now?

The only problem is to avoid a trump loser. In theory the odds heavily favour the finesse, since there are still three spades outstanding. But in practice no thinking declarer will dream of taking the finesse, for West has announced to the world that he has the singleton king of trumps. Why else would he switch to hearts instead of leading a further diamond and giving his partner the chance to over-ruff dummy?

West clearly feared that his partner's inability to over-ruff dummy would give the show away and induce you to fell his singleton king. But in cases like this the defender gives the show away no matter what he does.

Elementary inferences such as this are quite common and

must not be missed. The next case is only slightly more complex.

```
♠ 9 8 7 5
♡ A Q 3            Game all
◇ Q J 6            Dealer North
♣ A 8 6            N        S
                   1 ◇      1 ♠
♠ A K J 3          2 ♠      3 ◇
♡ 7 6              3 ♠      4 ♠
◇ A 9 4 3
♣ 9 3 2
```

West leads the king of clubs which you allow to win the first trick. You win the continuation of the queen of clubs with the ace, lead a spade to your ace, and return a heart for a finesse of the queen. East produces the king and leads a club to his partner's knave, and West exits with a heart to dummy's ace.

There has been nothing but bad luck so far, but when you run the queen of diamonds East plays the five and West the two. You continue with the knave of diamonds, East playing the seven and West the ten. What is your next move?

The problem has been reduced to a choice between finessing or playing for the drop in trumps. If you give a little thought to the matter you will realize that the trump position has already been charted by East's play in the diamond suit. Holding the guarded queen of trumps, East would surely have covered the knave of diamonds, thereby locking you in hand and ensuring a trump trick for himself. You must therefore lead a trump to your king in the hope of dropping a doubleton queen.

In the final of the 1973 Vanderbilt competition, Bobby Wolff earned a swing for the Aces on this hand by drawing the correct inference and making his contract. East might have made the position harder to read, of course, by covering the first diamond.

There are certain hands on which the declarer must deliberately set out to obtain an inference from the play.

♠ Q 6 2
♡ K 10 3   • *Love all*
◇ K 9 8 3   *Dealer West*
♣ Q 7 4

W	N	E	S
1 NT (12–14)	—	2 ◇	2 ♡

♠ J 10 5   — | 3 ♡ | — | 4 ♡
♡ Q J 9 8 6 4   *All pass*
◇ —
♣ A J 6 2

West leads the ace of spades (he normally plays ace from ace-king), and on seeing his partner's three switches to the queen of diamonds. You play low from dummy and ruff in your hand. How should you continue?

With two losers in spades and one in trumps, you will need a bit of luck to make this contract. Not only must you find East with a singleton or doubleton king of clubs, but you must also arrange to ruff the fourth club in dummy.

If East has the ace of diamonds and the king of clubs West will have the ace of hearts, and if you lead a small trump he will no doubt play low in the hope that you have a guess to make. The trouble is that when dummy wins the trick you will not know how to continue. If you lead a second trump West may defeat you by taking the ace and returning a third trump. But if you play on clubs after one round of trumps East may be able to score a ruff.

You need to smoke out the ace of hearts on the first round, and the most likely way of achieving this is by leading the queen of trumps at trick three. Holding a doubleton ace, West is not likely to refuse the trick. If he plays the ace you will then be able to test the trump position before playing clubs. If West does play low on the queen of trumps, it is a fair indication that the trumps will be 3–1, and you should therefore overtake in dummy and play on clubs.

Valuable inferences can be drawn from the rank of the cards played. The opening lead is often a fruitful source of information.

♠ 8 4
♡ 6 4
◇ A Q 8 3 2   *Love all*
♣ A 10 7 3   *Dealer South*

	S	N
♠ K 9 2	1 ◇	3 ◇
♡ A K 7	3 NT	—
◇ K 10 6 4		
♣ K 6 5		

West leads the two of hearts, East plays the ten and you win the trick with the king. How should you continue?

There will be no difficulty in making nine tricks provided that you can bring in the diamonds without loss, and the cards are so distributed that you can score five tricks in diamonds even against a 4–0 break either way. All that you have to do is to determine which opponent is most likely to be void in diamonds.

The answer has already been provided by the opening lead. The two of hearts indicates that West has led from a four-card suit. Players tend to lead from their longest and strongest suit against a no trump contract, and it is therefore a safe inference that West does not possess a five-card or longer suit. From this it follows that his distribution can be no wilder than 4–4–4–1.

Only East can be void in diamonds, in that case, and you should lead the king of diamonds at trick two to cater for the possibility.

Many players echo to show distribution in certain situations, and some do it all the time. The normal procedure is to play low-high to show an odd number of cards and high-low to show an even number. These length signals can be of great help to the declarer in the play of the hand.

```
♠ 8 7 3
♡ Q 7 2
♢ K 7 6 4                   Love all
♣ 10 8 3                    Dealer South
                         S       N
♠ K Q 10 5              2 ♣     2 ♢
♡ J 6                   2 NT    3 NT
♢ A Q J
♣ A K Q J
```

West leads the four of hearts, East plays the ten and you win with the knave. How should you continue?

If the hearts are 4–4 you can safely establish the ninth trick by knocking out the ace of spades. Hearts might be 5–3, however, in which case the winning play could be to rely on a 3–3 diamond break. The trouble is that the plays cannot be combined to give a greater chance of success. If you overtake with the king of diamonds on the third round and a defender shows out, you will go down even with the hearts 4–4, for you will have established a fifth trick for the defence.

Nevertheless, you can obtain a good indication from the defenders if you handle the diamonds correctly. Lead the queen of diamonds at trick two and watch the small cards. Not knowing the location of the diamond ace, both defenders will be anxious to give honest information about the distribution of the suit. If the two of diamonds appears on the first round, therefore, you should assume that the suit is breaking evenly. After cashing the clubs you will continue with the ace of diamonds, then overtake the knave with the king and score the thirteenth diamond as your game-going trick.

If the opponents start an echo on the first round of diamonds, you should continue with the knave of diamonds to the king and try to slip past the ace of spades. As a last resort you have the chance of an even heart break.

The next hand illustrates the same theme in a more complex setting.

♠ K Q J 9 8 5 3
♡ K 5 2
◇ 8
♣ J 7

Love all
Dealer West

	W	N	E	S
	1 ♡	3 ♠	—	4 ♣
♠ 10 6	—	4 ◇*	—	4 ♡
♡ A 9 6 4	—	5 ♣†	—	6 NT
◇ A Q J	All pass			
♣ A K 5 2				

♠ 10 6
♡ A 9 6 4
◇ A Q J
♣ A K 5 2

* *No aces*   † *King of hearts*

West leads the queen of hearts, East plays the three and
you win with the ace. When you play the ten of spades West
follows with the four and East with the seven. What now?

There are eleven top tricks and it should be possible to
squeeze West in the red suits for the twelfth. The trouble is
that if you lead another spade at this point West is sure to
return a heart, removing dummy's entry and forcing you to
run the spades before you have a chance to rectify the timing
of the squeeze by cashing the top clubs.

West may have only two clubs, of course, and the play of
the king of clubs may produce some information. It does,
but the information is of little comfort. West plays the three
of clubs and East the nine. It appears that West has three
clubs and East four, in which case it cannot do any good to
cash the ace of clubs before leading another spade.

However, if West also has the queen of clubs he may be
subjected to a progressive squeeze in three suits. You should
therefore knock out the ace of spades, win the heart return
and run the spades, keeping three diamonds in your hand and
deliberately reducing your winner count from eleven to ten
by discarding the ace of clubs on the last spade. West will be
unable to withstand the pressure. If he discards his last heart
the five of hearts will squeeze him again. If he lets go the club
queen the knave of clubs will give him the business. And if he
bares the diamond king a diamond to the ace will bring in
the rest of the tricks.

This hand was played as described by Laszlo Kovacs in the Hungarian Team Championships of 1973 and reported by Gabor Salgo in the International Bridge Press Association Bulletin.

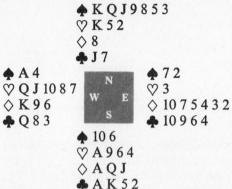

```
              ♠ K Q J 9 8 5 3
              ♡ K 5 2
              ◇ 8
              ♣ J 7
♠ A 4                        ♠ 7 2
♡ Q J 10 8 7       N         ♡ 3
◇ K 9 6        W     E       ◇ 10 7 5 4 3 2
♣ Q 8 3            S         ♣ 10 9 6 4
              ♠ 10 6
              ♡ A 9 6 4
              ◇ A Q J
              ♣ A K 5 2
```

It was perhaps a little naïve of East to signal his distribution on the play of the king of clubs. In a slam contract this is likely to help the declarer rather than partner.

However, the line of play chosen by Kovacs is correct no matter what happens on the first round of clubs. The opening bid marks West with all the key cards and the triple squeeze is bound to nail him. Here is the end position that was reached.

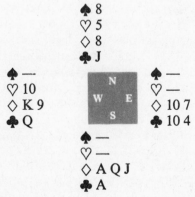

```
              ♠ 8
              ♡ 5
              ◇ 8
              ♣ J
♠ —                          ♠ —
♡ 10          N              ♡ —
◇ K 9     W       E          ◇ 10 7
♣ Q           S              ♣ 10 4
              ♠ —
              ♡ —
              ◇ A Q J
              ♣ A
```

South throws the ace of clubs on the last spade and West has to surrender.

```
♠ J 8 5 2
♡ 9 8 6 3          Game all
◇ J 10 7 2         Dealer South
♣ 5                S       N
                   2 ♣     2 ◇
♠ K Q              2 NT    3 ♣
♡ Q J 10           3 NT    —
◇ A K 6
♣ A K J 10 4
```

West leads the two of hearts and partner diffidently displays his pair of knaves. East wins the first trick with the ace of hearts and returns the nine of clubs, on which you play the ace. When you lead the queen of hearts West takes his king and returns a heart, on which East discards the ten of spades. You cash the king of clubs and continue with the knave to West's queen, discarding a diamond and a spade from the table. West leads the seven of spades to his partner's ace, and East returns the three of diamonds. How do you play?

At this stage you have eight top tricks, and you can play for the ninth either by trying to drop the queen of diamonds or by taking the finesse. Is it a guess? Only for those who refuse to think. Whether the diamond queen will drop or not there is every reason to believe that it is lurking in the West hand. Consider East's behaviour. Even if he is not capable of working out that you must have both the ace and king of diamonds, he would hardly offer you a free finesse by leading away from the queen when he could have exited safely in a black suit.

You should therefore play the ace of diamonds, cash your black winners, and follow with the king of diamonds. There should be a good chance that the queen will drop since East thought it worth while to offer you a losing option.

♠ K J 4
♡ J 7 6
♦ A Q J 6   *Game all*
♣ A K Q   *Dealer North*

	N	S
♠ A Q 8 7 6	2 NT	3 ♠
♡ 9 3 2	4 ♣	4 ♠
♦ 8 4		
♣ 10 5 2		

West leads the ace of hearts and his partner encourages with the ten. East wins the next heart with the queen and cashes the king, on which West discards the two of diamonds. East continues with a fourth heart. What do you make of that?

You have been given the opportunity to discard your losing diamond while ruffing in dummy. But should you accept it? It would be prudent to regard East's motives with suspicion. He is not out to do you any favours, you may be sure. The logical explanation for East's action is that he regards trumps as the only possible source of the setting trick. And that could mean that trumps will break badly. One thing is certain. East would never offer you a ruff and discard if he could see the king of diamonds in his own hand.

You will be able to cope with a 4–1 trump break provided that you do not block the suit. The trouble with discarding a diamond and ruffing in dummy is that West may have started with four trumps and three diamonds. If you discard a diamond on the fourth heart he will do the same. After ruffing in dummy and cashing the king and knave of trumps, you will have no entry to hand except through a diamond ruff. But West's king will drop under your ace and he will score a trump trick.

The correct play, therefore, is to ruff the fourth heart in hand. Whether West over-ruffs or not, you will then be able to cope with all the 4–1 trump breaks and make your contract with the aid of the diamond finesse.

♠ Q 8 5
♡ A 5 3
◇ A Q J 10 3   *Game all*
♣ 8 2   *Dealer North*
                          N   S
♠ K J 4   1 ◇   1 ♡
♡ K J 10 6 2   2 ♡   4 ♡
◇ K 9 7
♣ Q 5

West cashes the ace and king of clubs and then switches to the nine of spades. East wins with the ace and returns the four of hearts. How should you play?

There is nothing to worry about except the possibility of a trump loser, and East appears to have solved the problem for you with his helpful trump return. But such helpfulness must always be suspect. Do you really believe that East would go out of his way to give you a 'free' finesse in trumps if it was going to do you any good? He must surely realize that the defence needs a trump trick to defeat the contract, so why did he not exit passively in spades or diamonds and leave you to do the work yourself?

By far the most likely explanation is that East holds four trumps and realizes that any honour card his partner possesses must be a singleton. You should therefore resist the temptation to put in the ten or the knave of hearts on the first round. Instead you should play low and look for West's queen to pop up. If it does not, you will be no worse off than you would have been had East defended in more orthodox fashion.

As a general principle, the declarer should be reluctant to depart from his normal percentage play. When the opponents offer an alternative, it is likely that the normal play will succeed.

A defender will occasionally resort to subtle tactics in an attempt to conceal the true state of affairs.

♠ 7 6 4 2
♡ 10 7 2   *Game all*
♢ Q 10 3   *Dealer East*
♣ A 8 3   *W*   *N*   *E*   *S*
                                        1 ♠   Dbl
♠ K Q   2 ♣   —   2 ♠   3 ♡
♡ A K 9 8 4 3   —   4 ♡   *All pass*
♢ K J 5
♣ K Q

The lead of the ten of spades goes to the ace, and East returns the three of spades. West ruffs your king with the five of hearts and switches to the knave of clubs. How do you plan the play?

If East is going to ruff this trick you are down for sure, so forget about that possibility. But if East is not void in clubs there is something fishy about his lead of the three of spades at trick two. What can he be up to? Holding the ace of diamonds, as he must on the bidding, why did he not return a high spade to ask for the diamond lead that would have enabled him to push another spade through?

There can be only one logical answer to that question. East was looking at all the outstanding trumps and did not wish to regain the lead with the ace of diamonds, knowing that his next lead would then give the show away whether he played a spade or not.

You should therefore play the ace of clubs from dummy at trick four. If it is not ruffed you will lead a trump and take the deep finesse when East plays low. If East splits his honours, you will be able to create an entry in diamonds in order to repeat the finesse.

♠ A Q 8 7 5 3
♡ 10 9 3   *N–S game*
◇ 7   *Dealer North*
♣ A Q 7   W   N   E   S
                                     1 ♠   2 ♣   3 ♡
♠ J 2   —   3 ♠   —   4 ♡
♡ A K Q J 7 6 4   —   5 ♣   —   6 ♡
◇ K Q 4   *All pass*
♣ 5

In an expert game you land in six hearts and receive the
lead of the ace of diamonds. East follows with the three, and
after a look at dummy West continues with the eight of
diamonds to the nine and king. When you draw trumps East
throws the two of clubs on the second round. How should
you continue?

There is a straightforward play for the contract by taking
the spade finesse. On the bidding East could well have both
black kings, however, and an attractive alternative is to play
for a black suit squeeze. First you would have to unblock the
spades by means of a Vienna Coup, leading a spade to the
ace and then running the trumps and cashing the queen of
diamonds to squeeze East.

That seems the best line until you reflect that West had the
opportunity to break up the entries for this squeeze by
switching to a club at trick two. Why did he not do so? It
may have been carelessness, but in an expert game it is wise
to assume that the opponents are defending to the best of
their ability. The chances are that West had a sound reason
for leaving you with the option of the squeeze, and what
reason could be sounder than the possession of the king of
spades? You should therefore lead a club to the ace and ruff
a club, and if the king does not drop fall back on the spade
finesse.

When this hand turned up in the 1970 European Cham-

pionships at Estoril the declarer got it wrong, playing for the
losing squeeze instead of the winning finesse.

♠ 9 4
♡ K 4 2   *Game all*
◇ K 9 4 3   *Dealer South*
♣ J 8 6 5   S   N
                    2 ♠   2 NT
♠ A K Q 10 7   3 ◇   4 ◇
♡ 6   4 ♠   5 ◇
◇ A J 10 5   6 ◇   —
♣ A K 3

West leads the queen of hearts and you play low from the
table. After a little thought, East plays the ace of hearts and
switches to the five of spades. You play the ace and West
follows with the six. You cash the ace of diamonds and run
the knave successfully, both opponents following suit. What
now?

Having guessed the trump position, you are well placed to
make your shaky slam. A 4–2 spade break will see you home.
Alternatively you can combine chances in the black suits by
cashing the top clubs, entering dummy with a third trump,
discarding your losing club on the king of hearts and ruffing
a club. If the queen of clubs does not appear, you still have
the chance of 3–3 spades or a doubleton knave.

But we have not yet taken account of East's strange action
in overtaking the queen of hearts in order to return a spade.
Surely he would do this only if he thought his partner would
be able to ruff, and that means he must have five spades in
his own hand. This inference is so strong that you should
reject all the other chances in favour of entering dummy with
a third trump and finessing the ten of spades.

This hand comes from the 1973 European Championships
at Ostend, and again the declarer got the position wrong.
Even at championship level simple inferences are often
missed.

East was suffering from an excess of zeal, of course. If the declarer *has* six spades he will still go down if East plays low to the first trick.

♠ Q 5
♡ A K J
◇ K 10 9 4   *N–S game*
♣ 8 7 5 3   *Dealer South*

	S	W	N	E
♠ 9 7 4	1 NT	2 ♠	3 ♠	—
♡ 10 6 3	4 ◇	—	5 ◇	All pass
◇ A Q J 8				
♣ A K Q				

West begins with the ace and king of spades, and you are thankful to have avoided three no trumps. Seeing his partner's echo, West continues with the ten of spades. You ruff in dummy with the nine of diamonds, and East surprises you by under-ruffing with the two of diamonds. When you draw trumps West shows out on the second round, discarding two spades. How should you continue?

The straightforward line of play is to test the clubs by playing three rounds. If the suit fails to break 3–3 you can always fall back upon the heart finesse.

But you have yet to account for East's odd behaviour. What can be the explanation of that under-ruff? The only one that appears to make sense is a holding of three hearts headed by the queen, four diamonds and four clubs. In that case East was squeezed at trick three and a trump was the only card he could spare.

The presence of the ten of hearts in your hand suggests a line of play that will succeed against this distribution. You should lead a heart to the king, return to the queen of clubs, cash the king of clubs and then lead your last trump, discarding the knave of hearts from the table. East will be caught in a criss-cross squeeze. If he throws a club you will cash the ace of clubs to make dummy high. And if he parts with a heart you can expect to drop the queen by leading to the ace of hearts.

Although this line of play is clearly indicated it carries no absolute guarantee of success. A tricky player in the East seat may have set out to create an illusion in your mind by under-ruffing when holding three or four small hearts. Fortunately not many defenders play as well as that.

♠ 10 9 3			
♡ K 4			
◇ 8 6 5 3		*Love all*	
♣ A K Q 2		*Dealer West*	
	W	*N*	*E*	*S*
♠ A K Q 8 5	1 ◇	—	1 ♡	1 ♠
♡ 10 7 2	4 ♡	4 ♠	*All pass*	
◇ 4			
♣ 9 8 5 4			

West begins with the ace and king of diamonds, his partner following with the ten and queen. You ruff the second diamond and lead a heart which West wins with the ace. He continues with the knave of diamonds, East discards the three of clubs and you ruff. How should you continue?

You can afford to lose one more trick, but your contract is vulnerable against a bad trump break now that you are reduced to three trumps. West is marked with six diamonds and four hearts, which makes it a certainty that one of the black suits will break badly. After ruffing a heart in dummy you could cope with a 4–1 trump break by drawing no more than one round of trumps and playing on clubs. But it would be fatal to allow West to ruff a club when he has a small doubleton trump, for a diamond return would force you again and promote a trick for the knave of spades.

The clue to the right line of play lies in East's discard of a club on the third diamond. East would discard a club from three or from five, but with four clubs he would surely discard a heart. The dangerous holding of two spades and one club in the West hand is therefore not at all likely. A further point is that West might have led a singleton club if he had one.

The correct play at this point is a club just in case West is void. If he ruffs he will be ruffing a loser, and you will be able to ruff the diamond return, draw trumps in two rounds and claim the remainder. If West discards on the club, you can cash the king of hearts, return to hand with a trump, ruff a heart and draw trumps, conceding a club at the end.

If West follows to the first club, you should cash the king of hearts, play a trump to hand, ruff a heart, and then play clubs until East ruffs. The remaining trump in dummy protects against the danger of a heart force.

The full hand:

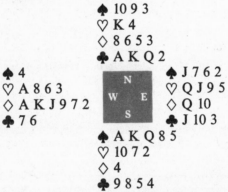

```
              ♠ 10 9 3
              ♡ K 4
              ◇ 8 6 5 3
              ♣ A K Q 2
♠ 4                              ♠ J 7 6 2
♡ A 8 6 3                        ♡ Q J 9 5
◇ A K J 9 7 2                    ◇ Q 10
♣ 7 6                           ♣ J 10 3
              ♠ A K Q 8 5
              ♡ 10 7 2
              ◇ 4
              ♣ 9 8 5 4
```

Again one sees deceptive possibilities for the defence. If East had held a club more and a spade less he might have lured you to defeat by discarding a club on the third diamond.

5. Retaining an Option

The expert declarer can usually be recognized by the way in which he organizes his sequence of play so as to take full advantage of all the options that are available. Needing to develop an extra trick, he will test one possibility after another in logical order so that failure at any stage but the final one will not automatically result in the defeat of the contract.

Although he is better at guesswork than most players, the expert hates to have to guess and will take great pains to avoid making an early decision in a critical suit. Before committing himself he will attempt to find out all he can about the distribution of the hand, first looking for a favourable break in one suit, then investigating the lie of another. When all other possibilities have been exhausted he may fall back on a finesse.

This cautious approach has much to commend it, for in the early stages of the play the declarer does not know enough about the hand to take critical decisions with any degree of confidence. On many hands it is only by testing one suit that he can discover how many tricks he needs from another.

Bridge would be an easier game if you could plan the play of the hand in a vacuum, without having to worry about interference. But in real life you do not have undisputed control of the play. Aggressive opponents sit on each side of you, brooding darkly and biding their time. As soon as they gain the lead they try to damage your prospects, and one good way of doing this is by attacking your options.

The defenders are handicapped by lack of knowledge of the size and disposition of their forces, but they have a compensating advantage. From the moment that dummy goes down they know all about your bad breaks, which is something you may not discover until much later. Defenders soon learn to trade upon your ignorance in this respect by forcing you to make premature decisions. A common stratagem is to compel you to take or reject a critical finesse before you know whether your side suit will or will not break kindly. Faced with such a guess, you are bound to do the wrong thing some of the time.

Another way in which the defenders may make a nuisance of themselves is by forcing you to take a discard before you know which card can be spared from your hand. In such a situation you would normally wish to postpone your discard until a later stage in the play. An established winner in dummy opposite a void in your hand can act like a sword hanging over the heads of the defenders, who may be inhibited from holding up in another suit for fear of losing their trick altogether. As soon as the winner is cashed and a discard taken, however, the threat is dissipated and one of your options vanishes.

You must therefore consider carefully what damage a defender may be able to inflict when he gains the lead. The best percentage play in a particular suit may have to be rejected simply because its failure would allow an opponent to attack one of your options, thus reducing the chance of success for the hand as a whole.

The easiest hands are those on which there is no question of losing an early trick to the opponents. Then the technique of preserving options is just a matter of playing your cards in the right order.

Here is an example.

♠ 7 2
♡ Q 6
◇ A K 10 9 4 3   *Game all*
♣ A J 6   *Dealer North*
                            N   *S*
♠ K 9 4   1 ◇   2 NT
♡ K 10 2   3 NT   —
◇ Q 5
♣ K 8 7 5 2

West leads the six of spades and you capture East's queen with your king. How should you plan the play?

There will be no problem if the diamonds break 3–2 or if the knave is singleton, for that will give you six diamond tricks, two clubs and one spade. The hand will become awkward if an opponent turns up with a diamond stopper, however. You cannot afford to concede a trick to the knave of diamonds, since that would allow the defenders to cash at least five winners.

The club suit offers an alternative source of tricks. By finessing against the queen it may be possible to score five tricks in the suit, which, together with three diamonds and a spade, will see you home.

But if you play the diamonds in normal fashion by cashing the queen and leading small to the king, you will find yourself badly placed if an opponent shows out on the second round. You will need to take a first-round club finesse but will be unable to do so because you are in the wrong hand.

To retain the option of trying for five club tricks, therefore, you must lead your small diamond to the ace or king at trick two and return a diamond to the queen. Then you will be poised to take advantage of a favourable club position if it proves necessary to do so.

A moment of carelessness could deprive you of one of your options on the next hand.

♠ Q 10 9 5
♡ Q 6 3
◇ K J 5 4   *Game all*
♣ 8 2   *Dealer South*
                    S   N
♠ J   1 ♡   1 ♠
♡ A 9 7 2   2 NT   3 ♡
◇ A Q 8 3   3 NT   —
♣ A K 7 5

West leads the three of clubs, East puts in the ten and you win the trick with the king. When you lead the knave of spades West follows with the six and East with the four. How should you continue?

It may not be easy to score a second spade trick now that the knave has been allowed to win. You will need three entries to dummy, two to establish the spades and a third to cash the winner. The alternative play for the contract is to hope for the king of hearts to be well placed. However, on a normal diamond break you should be able to create the three entries that you need by unblocking your eight of diamonds under the knave and your queen of diamonds under the king.

What you must not do is lead the eight of diamonds to the knave at trick three and continue with a spade from the table, for that commits you irrevocably to the 3–2 diamond break. When the opponents win the second spade a club will come back, and if the diamonds subsequently prove to be 4–1 you will be left with no way of preventing the defenders from making five tricks.

A slight adjustment to the sequence of play is all that is required. At trick three you should cash the ace of diamonds before leading the eight to dummy's knave. The difference is that you will then learn about the diamond break in good time. If the diamonds are 3–2 you can carry on with your plan to establish a second spade trick. If diamonds prove to

be 4–1 you can abandon spades and fall back on the chance
of finding the king of hearts with West.

♠ A 3
♡ K 8 4
◇ 9 8 6 5 3   *Game all*
♣ Q J 5   *Dealer South*
                      S   *N*
♠ K 6   1 NT   3 NT
♡ A Q 7 3
◇ A J 10 7
♣ K 7 2

West leads the queen of spades against your contract of
three no trumps. How do you plan the play?

You have six top tricks and need to develop three more.
One possibility that immediately suggests itself is to take a
double finesse in diamonds, a play that will always produce
nine tricks unless West has both king and queen of diamonds.
The alternative play is to knock out the ace of clubs and rely
on a 3–3 heart break for the ninth trick.

The choice between the two lines of play is not at all close.
The double finesse in diamonds gives a 76 per cent chance
of success against 36 per cent for the even heart break.

But of course there is no need to make a choice at this
stage, for you can keep both options open while testing the
lie of the cards. The correct play is to win the first trick in
hand with the king of spades, cash the ace and queen of
hearts, and continue with a heart to the king. This will give
you all the information you need to determine which suit to
tackle. If the hearts break 3–3 you will make your contract
in comfort by knocking out the ace of clubs. If the hearts fail
to break you must rely on the double diamond finesse, and
you are in the right hand to tackle the suit.

By playing the cards in the proper order you increase the
overall chance of success to nearly 85 per cent.

♠ A 6
♡ Q 10 6 3
◇ J 7 2   *Love all*
♣ A Q J 8   *Dealer South*

                           S   N
♠ K Q 2   1 NT   2 ♣
♡ K 7 5   2 ◇   3 NT
◇ Q 8 6
♣ K 6 5 4

West leads the knave of spades and you win in dummy
with the ace. How should you continue?

There are seven tricks in the black suits and, since you
cannot afford to open up the diamonds, you must hope to
make two tricks in hearts. The natural play at trick two
appears to be a low heart to the king, but if West produces
the ace and continues spades you will find yourself awk-
wardly placed.

Ideally, you will want to cater for a doubleton knave in the
East hand by leading a heart to the queen, returning to the
king of clubs, and leading a third heart. But the entry position
makes this impossible. If you do not cash the queen of spades
before leading the third heart you may never make it, while
if you do cash the queen of spades the enemy will score too
many tricks.

You will therefore be reduced to making a critical decision
on the third round of hearts, either finessing the ten and
risking losing to a doubleton knave, or playing the queen and
another heart in the hope of a 3–3 break.

All this trouble can be avoided by leading the queen of
hearts from the table at trick two. This play preserves all the
options in the heart suit, and the contract will be defeated
only when East has four or more hearts including the knave.

♠ K Q J 4
♡ A K 8   *Game all*
◇ 10 5   *Dealer South*
♣ A J 10 2   *S   N*
                          1 NT   2 ♣
♠ A 7   2 ♡   4 ♣
♡ Q 7 6 4   4 ◇   6 NT
◇ A Q 8 3
♣ K 9 5

West leads the nine of spades and you win in dummy with
the king. How should you continue?

Clubs should be tackled first, for a correct guess in clubs
will solve all your problems. Even if the club finesse loses
you will have eleven tricks and good chances for the twelfth
in one of the red suits.

Considering the club suit in isolation, the best play is to
lead small to the king and finesse on the way back. This
succeeds whenever West has the queen and also when East
has the queen singleton. But do you see what will happen if
you adopt this line of play and the finesse loses? Any sort of
bridge player in the East seat will return a diamond whether
he holds the king or not. This will destroy one of your
options by forcing you to make a premature choice between
the diamond finesse and the even heart break.

Such a dilemma must be avoided when possible, and you
should therefore play the clubs the other way, giving up the
chance of dropping a singleton queen and leading the two of
clubs to your nine. If this holds the trick you can unblock
the ace of spades, return to dummy in hearts, and repeat the
finesse by running the knave of clubs. If the finesse loses
West will be unable to make a damaging return from his side
of the table and you will have time to test the hearts for an
even break. If all else fails you can resort to the diamond
finesse.

♠ A 7 6 3
♡ 10 8 5 2
◇ K 8 2   *Game all*
♣ K 2   *Dealer South*

	S	N
♠ 5 4	1 ♡	3 ♡
♡ A Q 7 6 4	4 ♡	—
◇ A J 6		
♣ Q 8 4		

West leads the queen of spades against your contract of four hearts. How do you plan the play?

You are faced with a certain loser in each black suit, a possible loser in diamonds, and one or two possible losers in trumps. It is often correct to duck the first trick in a side suit in order to sever the enemy communications, but this is not the proper occasion for such a move. The trouble with ducking is that East may overtake with the king of spades and shoot back a trump, putting you to a guess before you know if you can afford a trump loser or not.

In order to find out how to tackle the trumps you must first clarify the diamond position. The correct play is the ace of spades at trick one followed by a diamond to your knave. If the finesse succeeds you will know that you can afford to lose a trump trick and will therefore cash the ace of hearts at trick three. This is the safety play to guard against losing two trump tricks when West has the singleton king. If nothing significant drops under the ace of hearts you will continue with a club to the king and eventually lead a second trump from the table.

If the diamond finesse loses, of course, you will need to pick up the trumps without loss. When dummy regains the lead you will play a trump and finesse the queen.

♠ 6
♡ A Q 9 3   *Game all*
◊ 7 5   *Dealer North*
♣ A K J 10 4 3   *N*   *S*
                              1 ♣   1 ♡
♠ K 10 7 4   4 ♡   4 NT
♡ K J 10 8 2   5 ♡   6 ♡
◊ A 8 3
♣ 7

West leads the queen of diamonds and you win the trick
with the ace. How should you plan the play?

You appear to be at full stretch on this hand, although the
slam has a fair chance of success. Given reasonable breaks it
should be possible to discard your diamonds and some of
your spades on the established clubs. If the clubs break 3–3
you will have four discards and can afford the trumps to be
3–1. If clubs break 4–2, on the other hand, you will be able
to discard only two diamonds and one spade and will need to
find a 2–2 trump break.

A little care is needed in order to keep both options open.
Suppose you lead a club to the ace, ruff a club, and enter
dummy with a trump. Now you will not know how best to
proceed. If you ruff another club and re-enter dummy with a
trump, you may find the trumps 3–1 when the clubs were 3–3
all the time. Alternatively if you draw a second round of
trumps you may find trumps 2–2 but clubs 4–2, in which case
you will be unable to establish the clubs in time for lack of a
quick entry to dummy.

The way to cater for both chances is to cash the ace *and*
king of clubs before ruffing a club. With the club position
exposed, you will know just what you need to play for in the
trump suit.

♠ K 4
♡ A 2   *Game all*
◇ A 8 6   *Dealer South*
♣ A K 9 7 6 5   S   N
                         1 ♠   3 ♣
♠ A Q J 7 6   3 ♡   4 ♣
♡ Q 9 8 6 4   4 ♡   6 ♠
◇ K 2
♣ 4

West leads the ten of diamonds and you win in hand with the king. Both opponents follow suit when you lead a trump to the king and return a trump to the ace, but on the queen of spades West discards the five of diamonds. You throw the eight of diamonds from dummy on this trick. How should you continue?

The 4–2 trump break complicates the hand a little, but if the clubs break no worse than 4–2 you should be able to establish enough winners by conceding a club and then ruffing a club. It would be a mistake to rely entirely on the club suit, however. There will still be a chance of making twelve tricks by playing on hearts even if the club suit breaks 5–1.

What you cannot afford to do at this stage is to draw the last trump, for you do not know whether you should discard a heart or a club from dummy. Instead you must immediately test the clubs by playing to the ace and cashing the king. If both opponents follow suit, you will concede the next club trick and retain control.

If East ruffs the second club you will over-ruff. A heart to the ace and a heart back will then bring in twelve tricks if East started with three hearts headed by the king.

In the last two examples it was right to cash the top cards in the side suit as a form of discovery play. This is not always the case, however.

♠ 9 3
♡ K Q 9 4   *Love all*
◇ 7 2   *Dealer North*
♣ A K 7 6 3
                   N   S
                   1 ♣   1 ♡
♠ K 8 2   2 ♡   3 ◇
♡ A J 10 8 5 3   4 ♡   6 ♡
◇ A J 6
♣ Q

West leads the king of diamonds which you win with the ace. Both opponents follow suit when you cash the ace of hearts, and your next move is to unblock the queen of clubs. When you lead a heart to the king West discards the three of diamonds. What now?

On a normal 4–3 club break it will be possible to discard all your spades. You can then concede a diamond and ruff your last diamond in dummy. If the clubs break 5–2, however, the only plan with a chance of success will be to discard two diamonds on the top clubs and play for the ace of spades to be right. Which plan do you choose?

Once again there is no need to commit yourself quite so early. It would be a mistake to start discarding on the top clubs, for you do not yet know what to discard. The way to preserve your options for a little longer is to ruff a small club and return to dummy with the queen of hearts. The play of a top club may then give you the answer.

If East discards on the third round of clubs you will know that you have to discard diamonds from your hand and hope for East to have the ace of spades. If East follows to the third club, you cannot be sure of doing the right thing, but the percentage play will be to discard spades and hope for the club suit to break.

♠ A Q 7 5
♡ K Q 6 2
♢ 7 4   *N–S game*
♣ K Q 4   *Dealer East*

	W	N	E	S
♠ K J 10 8 6 3 2			3 ♣	3 ♠
♡ J 9	5 ♣	6 ♠	*All pass*	
♢ A Q 9 2				
♣ —				

West leads the nine of clubs against your contract of six spades. How do you plan the play?

On the lead East is marked with the ace of clubs, which means that both the ace of hearts and the king of diamonds will be with West. You need to find a way of avoiding one of those losers, and it may occur to you that you will be able to get all your diamonds away if you can persuade West to beat air with the ace of hearts.

Suppose that the play to the first trick goes: king of clubs, ace, and ruff. After drawing trumps you can catch West on the horns of a dilemma by leading the nine of hearts. If he takes his ace, you will have two discards on hearts and one on the queen of clubs to take care of your losing diamonds. If West ducks the first heart, you can exercise the option to discard your remaining heart on the established queen of clubs. After conceding a diamond trick you can then claim your slam.

There is just one flaw in the above analysis. We are assuming too readily that East will co-operate by playing the ace of clubs on the first trick. Most players will, it is true, but a thinking defender will realize that you are going to obtain a discard on the clubs anyway and may exercise *his* option by playing low to make you take your discard at an inconvenient time.

This defence will sabotage your plan completely, for there is no satisfactory discard that you can make at trick one.

Your choice of discard is dependent on whether West plays the ace of hearts or a small heart when the suit is led, and it cannot be made prematurely. If you are forced to find a discard at trick one you will be unable to avoid two losers.

There is no need to put yourself in this position, of course. You can make your slam a near certainty by playing a low club from dummy at trick one. East will then have no way of compelling you to take a discard at the first trick. You will ruff in hand, draw a round of trumps with the king and a second round if necessary with the knave, and lead the nine of hearts to catch West in the familiar dilemma. If he plays the ace, you will have enough discards to take care of all your losing diamonds.

If East ducks the first heart you will ruff out the ace of clubs, enter dummy in trumps, and discard your knave of hearts on the queen of clubs. At this point, if spades were 2–0, you will have only one trump left in dummy, but the slam will still be safe if West has no more clubs. Just lead a diamond and cover East's card as cheaply as possible. Any red suit return from West will yield the twelfth trick.

The full hand:

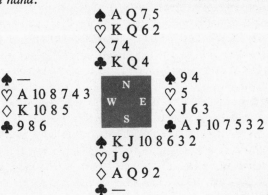

♠ A Q 7 5
♡ K Q 6 2
◇ 7 4
♣ K Q 4

♠ —
♡ A 10 8 7 4 3
◇ K 10 8 5
♣ 9 8 6

♠ 9 4
♡ 5
◇ J 6 3
♣ A J 10 7 5 3 2

♠ K J 10 8 6 3 2
♡ J 9
◇ A Q 9 2
♣ —

The ace of hearts would have been a more fortunate choice of lead for West.

♠ A 8 5 4
♡ K Q 4 2   *Game all*
◇ A J 6   *Dealer South*
♣ 8 3
                  S   N
                 1 ♡   4 ♣*
♠ 7   4 NT   5 ♡
♡ A J 10 7 6 3   6 ♡   —
◇ Q 7 5 4
♣ A Q

> ** Swiss Convention denoting high card raise to 4 hearts*

West leads the queen of spades to dummy's ace. How should you plan the play?

The form of the problem should be familiar by now. If, after drawing trumps, you lead a diamond for a losing finesse of the knave, East will put you on the guessing griddle by returning a club whether he holds the king or not. You will thus lose one of your options at an early stage.

A much better line of play is to lead the six of diamonds from dummy on the first round of the suit. East cannot put up the king without giving you the contract, while if West captures your queen with the king he will have no damaging return to make. Whatever happens, you will not be forced to commit yourself in clubs before you know about the diamond break.

If the trumps are 2–1, however, you can do better still by playing on elimination lines. Ruff a spade high at trick two, return to dummy with a trump, and ruff another spade high. A further trump to dummy enables you to ruff the last spade, after which you can lead a diamond to the ace and return the six of diamonds to your queen. On this line of play you will make the contract whenever the diamonds are 3–3, when either defender has the king of diamonds singleton or doubleton, and also when the club finesse is right.

♠ 9 7 3
♡ A K 10 7   *Game all*
◇ A K 5   *Dealer North*
♣ K 8 3   N   S
                       1 ♡   1 ♠
♠ A J 10 8 2   2 NT   3 ♣
♡ J 6 3   3 ♠   4 NT
◇ 8   5 ♡   6 ♠
♣ A J 6 4

Pressing for points, you arrive in a dubious slam and receive the lead of the queen of diamonds. You win with the ace and run the seven of spades at trick two. West produces the queen of spades and continues with the knave of diamonds. Take it from there.

Naturally you must hope to pick up the king of spades by finessing again. Even then you will have only ten top tricks, but there will be chances for extra tricks in both hearts and clubs. What you cannot afford, however, is to make a discard at this point, for whatever you throw from your hand will reduce your chances in some way.

To keep your options open you must ruff this diamond lead (with the ten or knave in order to avoid a blockage). Then enter dummy with the ace of hearts and run the nine of spades to pick up the trumps. If trumps prove to be 4–1 you must discard a club from dummy on the fourth round and continue with your second low heart to the king. If the queen drops, one losing club can be discarded on the ten of hearts and the other on the king of diamonds.

If the queen of hearts fails to drop you will discard the knave of hearts on the king of diamonds. After a 3–2 trump break you can afford to ruff a heart at this point. If the suit proves to be 3–3 you can discard a club on the established heart and then take the club finesse. If hearts fail to break, or if the trumps were 4–1, you will need to find the clubs 3–3 as well as the queen with East.

♠ 7 4
♡ J 8 7 6 4 2   *N–S game*
◇ K Q 9 6 5   *Dealer West*
♣ —

	W	N	E	S
	3 NT	—	5 ♣	5 ♠
♠ A K Q J 9 8 2	—	—	6 ♣	—
♡ A 10 3	—	6 ♠	*All pass*	
◇ J 8 4				
♣ —				

On inquiry you are informed that the opening bid of three no trumps indicates a solid minor suit with not more than a king outside. West leads the ace of clubs. How do you plan the play?

The natural thing to do is to ruff in dummy and throw a heart from hand. It is not too easy to see that any discard from your hand must destroy one of your options. East is marked with the ace of diamonds and it is likely that he will be able to hold up until the third round, thus denying you more than two diamond tricks. However, you will still have a chance of developing the heart suit, provided that you have not made the mistake of discarding a heart from your hand at trick one.

After ruffing the first trick in dummy, therefore, you should ruff again in your own hand. Then draw trumps, which you must hope to break no worse than 3–1, discarding two hearts from the table. Continue with the knave of diamonds and then a low diamond to the queen. If the diamonds are 3–2 East must hold off to create any problem, and now you can change horses by leading a heart from the table, putting in the ten if East plays low.

If the hearts are 2–2 with West holding one of the honour cards you are home, for your losing diamond will eventually be discarded on dummy's fourth heart.

♠ A K
♡ A K 10 3   *N–S game*
◇ Q 7 6 4   *Dealer West*
♣ A J 7   W   N   E   S
                        —   2 NT   —   4 ♠
♠ Q J 10 9 7 5 4   —   5 ♣   —   5 ◇
♡ Q 6 5 2   —   6 ♠   *All pass*
◇ —
♣ 10 3

The opening lead is the king of diamonds which you ruff.
When you tackle the trumps East discards a diamond on the
second round. How should you continue?

There will be no difficulty on a 3–2 heart break. Four
hearts in the West hand can also be easily dealt with, but the
contract could be at risk if East has a heart stopper. Is there
any way of catering for this distribution?

The twelfth trick would have to come from either a throw-
in or a squeeze. Prospects for a throw-in are dubious, because
you cannot afford to test the hearts before the last trump is
drawn. That means ruffing a diamond and finding a discard
from dummy on the third trump, which is likely to cut down
your options.

The menaces appear to be well placed for a double squeeze,
however. Remember that West, who passed originally, is
marked with the ace and king of diamonds. If the hearts are
breaking badly, West surely cannot have both club honours.
That would give him thirteen points, or twelve with a singleton heart and a five-card suit, on which he would have
opened the bidding.

To bring off a squeeze, of course, you will first have to
rectify the count by giving up a trick. The way to preserve all
your options on this hand is to lead the seven of clubs from
dummy at trick four. If West wins and returns a club you
will put on the ace. The queen of diamonds will then serve as
a menace against West and the knave of clubs as a menace

against East. When you ruff a small diamond and run the rest of the trumps neither opponent will be able to keep four hearts.

If East wins the first club he will have nothing better to return than a diamond. You will ruff and draw the last trump, discarding a heart from the table. The play of the ace and king of hearts will then expose the position. If East shows out, you can ruff the remaining small diamond and play your last trump, throwing the knave of clubs from dummy. A club to the ace will then squeeze West in the red suits.

If it is West who shows out on the second round of hearts, you have a different squeeze with clubs as the double menace. Win the third round of hearts with your queen and play out the trumps. West will have to keep the ace of diamonds and East the master heart, and neither will be able to guard the clubs.

One possible hand:

```
                    ♠ A K
                    ♡ A K 10 3
                    ◊ Q 7 6 4
                    ♣ A J 7
    ♠ 8 6 2                        ♠ 3
    ♡ 7                            ♡ J 9 8 4
    ◊ A K 9 5                      ◊ J 10 8 3 2
    ♣ K 8 5 4 2                    ♣ Q 9 6
                    ♠ Q J 10 9 7 5 4
                    ♡ Q 6 5 2
                    ◊ —
                    ♣ 10 3
```

6. Placing the Lead

In the last chapter we came across several hands on which the defenders could attack an option from one side of the table but not from the other. Manœuvring to keep a dangerous opponent off lead is a procedure that is familiar to all experienced players, and in this chapter we shall examine the theme in a more general setting.

After all, when an opponent succeeds in gaining the lead he will not be content to remove one of your options if he is in a position to inflict more direct damage on you. He may have the tricks in his hand to defeat the contract, for example, or he may be able to give his partner a ruff that you can ill afford. But perhaps the most common reason for attempting to concede a trick to one defender rather than the other is the desire to protect a tenace holding. The good declarer is a confirmed pessimist who has learned from experience that finesses frequently fail. It is therefore only logical for him to endeavour to lose a trick to the defender who is unable to lead through his tenaces.

A question of tempo arises on a certain type of hand. It may be safe to give up the lead to a particular defender at one stage in the play but dangerous later when his long suit has been established. When you have to let the defenders in more than once, therefore, you should first attack the entry that may lie in the danger hand.

Sometimes your best efforts to place the lead will gain no more than a small extra chance of success. At other times they will give you a sure play for the contract.

Consider the following example.

♠ Q 6 5
♡ 10 9 5 2
◇ A Q 7   *Game all*
♣ K 9 4   *Dealer South*

                                  S   *N*

♠ K 4 2   1 ♡   3 ♡
♡ A K Q 7 4   4 ♡   —
◇ 8 4 3
♣ A 6

West leads the knave of spades against your contract of four hearts. You play low from dummy, East puts in the seven and you win with the king. Both defenders follow suit when you cash the ace of trumps. How should you continue?

Three no trumps by North appears to be the ideal contract with nine tricks guaranteed. In four hearts you are in some danger of losing two spades and two diamonds. You will naturally assume that the diamond finesse is wrong and look for some means of avoiding it. Since East is marked with the ace of spades you should not have to look very far. It will always be possible to throw East in to lead diamonds for you, provided that you do not mess up the timing.

The safe way of making the contract is to draw the remaining trumps, eliminate the clubs by ruffing the third round, and then play a low spade from both hands.

The point is that you can afford to lose a spade trick to West as long as you do it before your exit card, the queen of spades, has gone. If West wins and leads another spade his partner will be end-played, compelled to open the diamonds or concede a ruff and discard. West cannot save the day by switching to diamonds, for you will simply play the ace and exit with the queen of spades. Again East will be forced to yield the tenth trick in one way or another.

♠ 10 7 3
♡ A 9 4 3
◇ A K 7 2   *Game all*
♣ 8 4   *Dealer South*
                              S   N
♠ A   1 ♡   3 ♡
♡ K Q J 8 5   4 ♡   —
◇ 8 6 5 4 3
♣ A Q

West leads the queen of diamonds, and when dummy goes
down you see that you have underbid the hand by a couple of
tricks. How do you plan the play?

Six hearts is the contract you would like to be in, and even
seven may be on. But your target is ten tricks and, as always
when the contract appears to be easy, you should look for
snags and play as safely as possible.

What can go wrong? The answer is obvious as soon as you
ask the question. East may be void in diamonds, in which
case he will welcome an opportunity to ruff the ace or the
king at trick one. A club will come back, and you will be
reduced to hoping that the king is well placed. If the king of
clubs is in the West hand you will go one or two down
depending on whether you take the finesse or not.

There is no need to put yourself in this position, of course.
The correct play is a low diamond from dummy at trick one.
If East shows out, you must keep up the good work by playing low on the second diamond as well. The contract is
always safe provided that you do not allow East to gain the
lead too early. You can afford to lose two diamonds and a
ruff, but not a club trick as well. When East ruffs the third
diamond and returns a club, you will play the ace, draw
trumps, and eventually discard the losing club in dummy on
your fifth diamond.

If East follows to the first diamond there is no danger, and

you can make sure of eleven tricks by playing high from
dummy on the second round.

♠ A 7 4
♥ Q 6 3
♦ K Q J 3   *Love all*
♣ J 10 2   *Dealer South*

	S	N
♠ K J 6	1 NT	3 NT

♥ A 10 9 5
♦ 10 7 6 4
♣ A 9

West leads the two of spades and you capture the nine
with your knave. How should you proceed?

The favourable lead has given you three spade tricks and
three more tricks can be developed in diamonds. Two heart
tricks and a club would bring your total up to nine. There is
danger in an immediate diamond lead, however. If East wins
and leads a club he is likely to set up at least three club tricks,
and the defenders will eventually score the setting trick in
hearts.

You should therefore attempt to lose the lead first to West,
since the clubs are immune to attack from that side of the
table. The best shot is to enter dummy with the ace of spades
and lead a low heart to your nine. If this draws the king you
have an easy play for nine tricks. If West wins with the knave
of hearts, you can win the spade return and knock out the
ace of diamonds. If East returns a club, your cause will not
now be hopeless. You can play the ace, cash your winning
diamonds, and eventually run the queen of hearts, making at
least nine tricks when East has the king.

There is one further variation. If East puts in the knave of
hearts on the first round of the suit it will probably be right
to assume that he has the king as well. You should therefore
win with the ace and switch to diamonds, hoping that the ace
of diamonds is with West.

♠ A 8 6 3
♡ —   *Match-point pairs*
◇ Q J 6 2   *Love all*
♣ A Q 8 4 3   *Dealer South*

	S	N
♠ 7 4	1 ♡	2 ♣
♡ A Q J 10 9 8 3	4 ♡	—
◇ A 5		
♣ K 5		

West leads the king of spades against your contract of four hearts. How do you plan the play?

The contract is in no danger, but the opening lead has attacked your weak spot and reduced the chance of overtricks. Twelve tricks will be possible only if clubs are 3–3 and the diamond finesse right. The odds against this combination are too long, and you should therefore limit your ambition to one overtrick.

It will take careful play to make even eleven tricks. You must make sure that East does not obtain the lead and shoot back a diamond before you have knocked out the king of trumps. At first glance it may appear adequate to win the first spade, come to hand with the king of clubs, and play the ace and queen of trumps. You could then win a diamond return with the ace, draw the outstanding trumps, and take your discard on the third club.

But the defenders need not be so co-operative. After winning the king of hearts and cashing their spade trick they may lead a second club, and you will again be reduced to playing for a 3–3 club break or taking the diamond finesse.

To give yourself the best chance of eleven tricks you must enter your hand with a third-round spade ruff. The correct play is to allow West to win the first trick. After winning the second spade, ruffing a spade high and playing the ace and queen of hearts, you will be able to cope with any return.

♠ Q J 7 5 2
♡ —   *N–S game*
♢ Q 6 5 2   *Dealer South*
♣ J 10 8 3   S   N
                                  2 ♣   2 ♢
♠ A 4   3 ♣   3 ♠
♡ A K 10   3 NT   5 ♣
♢ K 3   6 ♣   —
♣ A K 9 7 6 5

When West leads the four of hearts you discard a diamond
from dummy and capture the queen with your ace. On the
play of the ace of clubs East drops the queen. How should
you continue?

At first sight the slam appears to depend on the spade
finesse, but there are interesting possibilities in the diamond
situation. If you could manage to slip past the ace of diamonds, you could discard a further diamond from dummy on
the king of hearts and eventually throw in the defender who
holds the ace of diamonds. Clearly you must play West for
the ace of diamonds, since it would do you no good to throw
East in.

At trick three, therefore, you should lead the three of
diamonds from hand. If dummy's queen wins you can return
to hand with a trump, cash the king of hearts, discarding
another diamond from dummy, and ruff the ten of hearts on
the table. A diamond then throws the lead to West, who must
either open up the spades or give you a ruff and discard.

The slam is thus made not only when the spade finesse
works but also when West has the ace of diamonds. Clearly
it does West no good to go up with the ace when you lead the
three of diamonds, for your spade loser would then be
discarded on the queen of diamonds.

Note that you cannot afford to cash a second trump before
testing the diamonds. If you did you would have no way of

returning to hand without exhausting dummy of trumps and ruining the elimination:

```
♠ A K 4 2
♡ 7 6 4
♢ K 8 6            N–S game
♣ A J 5            Dealer West
                 W      N       E       S
♠ Q 9 7 6 5      1 ♡    Dbl     2 ♡     3 ♠
♡ K 8            —      4 ♠     All pass
♢ Q 9
♣ K 10 4 3
```

West leads the three of spades and East plays the ten under dummy's ace. When you continue with the king of spades East discards the two of diamonds. What now?

Your potential losers are two hearts, one diamond and one club, and it would clearly be unwise to put the contract at risk by taking the club finesse into the East hand. Your game is quite safe on the one reasonable assumption that West has the ace of diamonds. Once again the diamond position lends itself to an avoidance play.

The correct move at trick three is to run the knave of clubs from dummy. If West wins and returns a club, you can put up the ace, return to hand with the queen of trumps, and lead the nine of diamonds. West cannot gain by playing the ace, and when the king wins the trick you can play two more rounds of clubs and discard a diamond from dummy. Then put West on lead with the ace of diamonds, and he will have to return a heart or give you a ruff and discard.

This line of play is safe even if West is void in clubs, for if he ruffs he will have to lead a red suit to your advantage. But you cannot afford to cash the ace of clubs before running the knave. If West ruffed the ace of clubs he could exit by playing the ace and another diamond, and you would have no way of returning to dummy to enjoy your discard.

♠ 10 7 6 2
♡ Q 8   *Game all*
◇ 10 5 3   *Dealer South*
♣ A 10 9 4   S   N
                         2 NT   3 ♣
♠ A J 8   3 ◇   3 ♠
♡ A J 7   3 NT   —
◇ A Q J 8
♣ Q J 6

West leads the five of hearts against your contract of three
no trumps. The Rule of Eleven tells you that East has only
one heart higher than the five, so you try the queen from
dummy. This proves to be a wrong move when East produces
the king. How do you plan the play?

There are only five top tricks, and you need to develop
both the diamonds and the clubs to make your contract. You
could rely on one of the two finesses being right, but since
West appears to have the long hearts it must be better to
attack the potential entry in his hand first.

The correct play is to win the ace of hearts and play the ace
and another diamond, continuing the suit if necessary to
knock out the king. If a heart comes back you can allow
West to hold the trick as a safeguard against a 5–3 break.
The club finesse can then be taken in safety. If East produces
the king of diamonds and leads a spade, you can afford to go
up with the ace and tackle the clubs.

It would not be altogether safe to duck the first trick, for
East might switch to a spade. At that stage you would have
to play low and allow West to win, and no doubt a heart
would be returned. You would then find yourself in a guessing situation, uncertain whether to play West for one of the
minor suit kings by playing ace and another diamond or to
finesse in both minor suits. A wrong choice would cost you
the contract.

♠ A 4 3
♡ Q 6 2
◇ J 6 5   *Game all*
♣ 8 7 5 4   *Dealer South*
                              S   N
♠ K Q 5   2 NT   3 NT
♡ K 4
◇ A K 9 3 2
♣ A Q 6

West hits you in the weak spot with a lead of the nine of hearts. You play low from dummy, East plays the seven and your king wins the trick. How should you continue?

There are no more than seven top tricks, and you must hope to be able to develop two further tricks in diamonds without allowing West to gain the lead. That will be possible if East has any three diamonds, while if the queen is doubleton in either hand you will succeed in making an overtrick. Are there any other chances to be considered?

Well, you can also succeed if either opponent has a singleton queen of diamonds and if West has the singleton ten. But when East has the singleton queen, in order to place the lead in the right hand, you will have to let him hold the trick with it.

The proper play, therefore, is to cross to dummy with the ace of spades at trick two and lead a small diamond from the table. If the queen appears from the East hand you can allow it to win, and you will subsequently score four diamond tricks and your game. If East plays a small diamond, of course, you will put up the ace and continue with the king and another diamond.

Starting the diamonds from dummy improves your chance of success by no more than 2.8 per cent, but such an advantage can account for the difference between a winner and a loser.

♠ K
♡ J 10 3
◇ Q J 10 9 6 4   *Game all*
♣ 9 5 4   *Dealer South*

                    S   *N*

♠ A J 2   1 ♣   1 ◇
♡ A Q 7   3 NT   —
◇ K 5 2
♣ A J 8 3

West leads the six of spades, thereby removing the only
entry to the long diamonds. How do you plan the play?

There will be no difficulty if you can bring in the diamonds,
but if a defender has three diamonds headed by the ace he
will no doubt hold up until the third round and prevent you
from establishing the suit. There is no need to rely entirely on
the diamond suit, however, for there are other possible
sources of tricks. If you can score three heart tricks to put
alongside two spades and two diamonds, for instance, you
will need to develop just one extra trick from the clubs.

You should therefore reach the conclusion that the diamonds can wait. Since West can do no harm if he gains the
lead, it is safe to test the hearts first. Run the knave of hearts
at trick two, and if it wins continue with a heart to the queen.
If West produces the king you will have to rely on a 2–2
diamond break, but if the queen of hearts wins you can
continue with the king and another diamond. Suppose that
West shows out and East holds up his ace. You can then take
advantage of the entry to dummy to lead a low club towards
your eight. Provided that West has two of the outstanding
club honours, you will be able to establish a second trick in
the suit without allowing East to attack spades prematurely.

If you play on diamonds at trick two, you will find yourself
an entry short for your finesses and will have to tackle the
clubs from your own hand.

♠ 8 6 5 3
♡ J 10 4
◇ 7 5   *Love all*
♣ A K Q 3   *Dealer West*

	W	N	E	S
♠ A	1 ♠	—	2 ♠	3 ♡
♡ A Q 8 7 5 2	—	4 ♡	All pass	
◇ K 8 6 4				
♣ 8 4				

West leads the queen of spades to your ace. How do you plan the play?

On the bidding the heart finesse is sure to be wrong, which means that you will need to ruff at least one diamond in dummy to make the contract. The simplest way to prepare for this is to lead a diamond from hand at trick two. But the lead of a small diamond will give East the opportunity to win and shoot a trump through, and if West has three trumps headed by the king he will be able to remove the last trump from the table before you can ruff a diamond.

You need to place the lead in the West hand at trick two, and the correct card to lead is therefore the king of diamonds. On winning with the ace, West will be unable to attack the trumps with advantage. It does not matter if East wins the second diamond, for at that stage a trump lead will do no harm. You can win the second round of trumps, ruff a diamond, ruff a spade, draw the last trump, and discard your remaining diamond on the third club winner.

It would be a mistake to enter dummy in clubs at trick two in order to lead a diamond towards your king. Holding only two clubs, West could cut your communications by playing a second round of the suit. Then a trump lead from East when he is in with the second diamond would make the hand too difficult to manage.

♠ 10 9 3
♡ J 9 8
◇ K 10 3   *Game all*
♣ 9 7 6 2   *Dealer West*

	W	N	E	S
♠ K Q J 8 6 5 2	1 ♣	—	1 ♡	4 ♠
♡ A 10	All pass			
◇ A 6				
♣ K 5				

West leads the seven of hearts against your contract of four spades. East plays the queen and you win the trick with the ace. How should you continue?

In a sense you already have ten tricks—six spades, two hearts and two diamonds. It will not be easy to stop the defenders from scoring four tricks before you can make your ten, however. As soon as East gains the lead with the king of hearts, a club will come whistling through and down will go the contract. Is there any way of preventing East from gaining the lead?

On the bidding it is quite possible for West to have both the queen and the knave of diamonds, in which case you will be able to exchange your heart loser for a diamond loser. You have nothing to lose and perhaps a great deal to gain by trying for this chance. Before touching trumps, therefore, you should cash the diamond ace, lead a diamond to the king and return the ten of diamonds, discarding the ten of hearts if East does not cover. If West wins this trick he will be unable to put his partner on lead, and will have nothing better to do than play the ace and another trump.

You will win the second trump in dummy and lead the nine of hearts, ruffing out East's king and establishing a discard for one of your losing clubs.

♠ 8 5 2
♡ K 6 3   *N–S game*
◇ Q J 5   *Dealer East*
♣ A J 7 4   W   N   E   S
                                   1 NT (12–14)   2 ♡
♠ Q 10 3   —   3 ♡   —   4 ♡
♡ Q J 7 5 4   *All pass*
◇ A K 8 6
♣ 3

West leads the seven of spades to his partner's king. East cashes the ace of spades and continues with the six of spades to your queen, West following with the nine and the four. How should you continue?

Obviously you cannot stand a 4–1 trump break, but when the trumps are 3–2 you should be able to make the contract provided that you do not permit the defenders to get a trump promotion going. West appears to have led the middle card from a three-card spade holding, marking East with the thirteenth spade. You must therefore take care not to allow East to capture one of your trump honours on the first round of the suit.

If you lead a trump to the king and ace, for instance, the spade return will automatically promote a second trump trick for the defence. To guard against this danger you should enter dummy with the ace of clubs and lead a small trump from the table. If East beats air with his ace, a spade return will have no terrors for you. If East plays low and your queen wins, you must continue with the knave of hearts. You will then be safe against a spade return even if West started with three trumps.

East may not have the ace of hearts, of course, but this need not worry you since West is harmless on lead.

♠ 8 7 6 3
♡ A K   *N–S game*
◊ Q J 8 3   *Dealer East*
♣ A 7 4   W   N   E   S
                                1 ♡   2 ♣
♠ —   3 ♠   4 ♡   —   6 ♣
♡ 8 2   *All pass*
◊ A 6 5 4
♣ K Q 10 9 6 5 3

West leads the king of spades and his partner overtakes with the ace. You ruff and cash the king of clubs, both opponents following suit. How should you continue?

The opening bid marks the king of diamonds in the East hand, which means that there will be no problem on a normal 3–2 diamond break but that there may be complications if the diamonds are 4–1 or 5–0. However, your holdings in spades and diamonds are such that you should be able to place the lead with either opponent depending on how the play develops.

The correct procedure is to lead a club to the ace, ruff a spade, enter dummy with the ace of hearts and ruff another spade. Then re-enter dummy with the king of hearts and lead the queen of diamonds. If East covers with the king, win with the ace and lead another diamond. If West follows suit you can make sure of three diamond tricks by just covering his card. If West shows out on the first or second round of diamonds, you win the second diamond with the knave and lead the last spade from dummy, discarding a diamond from your hand. This places the lead with West, who will have to give you a ruff and discard.

If East does not cover the queen of diamonds on the first round, you return to hand by ruffing the last spade and lead a small diamond from your hand. If West shows out, the play of a low card from dummy will end-play East and ensure twelve tricks.

♠ Q 8 3
♡ 6 5 4 2
◇ A 8 4   *N–S game*
♣ K 8 7   *Dealer South*

	S	W	N	E
♠ A K 10 7 6 2	1 ♠	2 ♡	2 ♠	—
♡ 10 3	3 ♣	—	4 ♠	*All pass*
◇ 9				
♣ A 6 5 3				

West leads the knave of clubs and you win the trick with
the ace. How should you plan the play?

With two certain heart losers, you have to avoid losing
more than one trick in clubs. There will be no difficulty if the
clubs are 3–3, but the lead of the knave could well be from
shortage. It is tempting to start with a couple of rounds of
trumps. This will work admirably when the trumps are 2–2,
for you will then be able to ruff the fourth club at your
leisure. Testing the trumps could prove fatal when both black
suits break unevenly, however, for the defenders might be
able to stop you ruffing a club by playing a third round of
trumps.

Another idea that suggests itself is to return a club at trick
two, but this is not completely safe either. West might ruff,
put his partner in with a heart, and ruff another club. You
can afford the first ruff but not the second.

It is beginning to look as though the best approach must
be to cut the enemy communications by leading hearts. If you
lead hearts from your hand, however, there is no guarantee
that East will not be able to gain the lead twice in the suit and
give his partner two ruffs after all. But East is unlikely to have
more than one heart honour, in which case you can restrict
him to one entry in the suit by leading hearts from dummy.

The correct play is, therefore, a diamond to the ace and a
heart back. If East wins and returns a club West may be able
to ruff a loser, but that will not help the defence if East cannot

regain the lead. If East wins the first heart and returns a trump, you must win with the ace or king and lead your ten of hearts. You cannot afford to have the queen of spades removed from dummy before you have ruffed the fourth club.

Here is the distribution that you have to guard against.

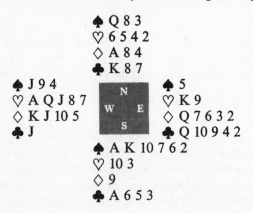

```
                    ♠ Q 8 3
                    ♡ 6 5 4 2
                    ◇ A 8 4
                    ♣ K 8 7
      ♠ J 9 4                        ♠ 5
      ♡ A Q J 8 7      N             ♡ K 9
      ◇ K J 10 5    W     E          ◇ Q 7 6 3 2
      ♣ J              S             ♣ Q 10 9 4 2
                    ♠ A K 10 7 6 2
                    ♡ 10 3
                    ◇ 9
                    ♣ A 6 5 3
```

Obviously the contract can be defeated on an initial trump lead.

7. Finding an Entry

Have you noticed that the expert player is seldom at a loss for an entry to establish or cash his winners? This does not happen by accident. The vital entry card that springs to hand just at the right moment is there because the expert foresaw the need for it at an early stage in the play—perhaps at trick one. By planning well in advance the expert makes sure that the entry card is preserved for use at the proper time.

Anticipation is the name of the game. Before playing a card the expert limbers up with a brief session of mental play, projecting the likely course of events upon the screen of his mind. In deciding how best to develop his tricks he works out the number of entries needed in each hand and counts them one by one. This exercise enables him to spot any blockage that may develop, and prevents him from embarking on a hopeless venture. It may also bring to light the need to create an extra entry in one hand or the other.

When crossing from hand to hand the expert is ever conscious of the need to unblock in order to keep the entry position as fluid as possible. At times the play of the hand seems to consist of an endless series of small unblocking plays, most of which prove to be unnecessary. But once in a while an unusual distribution will appear, and then the automatic unblocking play will pay for its keep by providing an extra entry where it is most needed.

Every experienced player knows the value of the gambit in creating an entry where none existed before. A defender is offered an early trick in exchange for a later entry that may be worth two or three tricks. Often the defender is unable to refuse the gift without abandoning all chance of a trick in the suit. Here is a typical example.

♠ K Q 7 6 2
♡ 6 5   *N–S game*
◇ 5 2   *Dealer East*
♣ 10 6 4 3   *W*   *N*   *E*   *S*

                                   1 ♠   Dbl
♠ —   2 ♠   —   —   3 ♡
♡ A K 9 8 4 3   *All pass*
◇ J 9 8
♣ A K J 7

West leads the three of spades to the king and ace, and you win the first trick by ruffing. The nine of diamonds is won by West with the ten, and the two of hearts is returned to the queen and king. How should you continue?

Assuming a 3–2 trump break, you are still in danger of losing a trump, three diamonds and a club. Your attempt to ruff a diamond in dummy is likely to prove futile, for the defender who next gains the lead will surely return another trump.

The chances of dropping a doubleton queen of clubs are not good, but it is likely that the clubs will break 3–2. This may suggest a way of gaining access to the stranded queen of spades, in which case you will feel grateful for the initial spade lead.

The gambit has to be made while dummy still has a trump to guard against the run of the diamonds. Before cashing a second trump, therefore, you should lead the knave of clubs from hand. If the suit breaks 3–2 the defenders will be unable to duck without giving up their club trick. If an opponent takes the queen of clubs, you will win the trump return, cross to dummy with the ten of clubs, and discard one of your losing diamonds on the queen of spades.

```
♠ A Q 7 5
♡ K 10                  Game all
◇ A K J                 Dealer North
♣ A 9 4 3               N        S
                        2 NT     3 ♡
♠ 6                     3 NT     4 ◇
♡ A Q J 9 6 3           4 ♡      4 NT
◇ 10 9 8 5 2            5 ♠      6 ♡
♣ 7
```

West leads the knave of spades and East drops an en-
couraging nine under the ace. When you cash the king of
hearts East startles you by discarding the three of spades.
How should you continue?

Fortunately your trump holding is such that you can
afford to overtake dummy's ten on the second round. After
drawing trumps you will be left with only one trump in your
hand, however, and you should therefore consider carefully
how best to tackle the diamonds.

There will be no problem if the diamonds break 3-2 provided that you do not block the suit by taking a losing finesse.
If either defender has four diamonds headed by the queen,
however, it will not be good enough to play the ace, king and
knave of diamonds after drawing trumps. The killing defence
of a low diamond on the third round will leave you with no
way back to hand except by using your last trump.

The hand is really a straightforward exercise in unblocking.
In order to cater for the possibility of a 4–1 diamond break
you must cash one top diamond at trick two and then draw
the remaining trumps, discarding the other two diamonds
from dummy. The lead of the ten of diamonds then knocks
out the queen and you take the rest of the tricks.

This line of play fails only when West is void in diamonds,
in which case there is never any play for the contract.

♠ 10 6 3
♡ K 4   *Love all*
♢ K 10 6   *Dealer South*
♣ A K 9 8 2   S   N
                 1 ♡   2 ♣
♠ A J 5   2 ♡   3 ♢
♡ A Q 10 8 5   3 NT   —
♢ 5 4
♣ J 6 4

West leads the king of spades and East follows suit with
the two. You win with the ace and lead the four of clubs, on
which West plays the five. In view of the shaky diamond
position it seems a good idea to develop the clubs without
allowing West to gain the lead, so you put in dummy's eight.
To your surprise and joy East follows with the three. How
should you continue?

Four club tricks, two spades and three hearts would see
you home, but you still cannot afford to concede a club trick
to West. Two diamond leads from his side of the table might
enable the defenders to score far too many tricks. However,
since West is marked with the queen and ten of clubs it
should be possible to score *five* club tricks even if the suit
breaks 4–1. All you need are two entries to hand in order to
finesse twice in clubs.

At trick three, therefore, you should lead the ten of spades
from the table. If West wins with the queen, the knave of
spades will serve as an extra entry to your hand and you will
make at least ten tricks.

West is more likely to allow the ten of spades to win, of
course, in which case both your entries will need to come
from the heart suit. Play the king of hearts from dummy and
overtake with the ace in order to lead the knave of clubs.
This sacrifices one of your heart tricks, but ensures five club
tricks and the contract in return.

♠ J 5
♡ A 8 3
◇ 7 4   *Game all*
♣ A J 10 9 4 2   *Dealer South*
                 S   N

♠ A Q 6 4   2 NT   4 NT
♡ K Q 7   6 NT   —
◇ A Q J 6
♣ K 7

The opening lead is the knave of hearts and you win in hand with the king. How do you plan the play?

There will be no problem if you can bring in the club suit without loss. That will give you twelve or thirteen tricks depending on whether you take the right finesse at the end. But if a club trick has to be lost you will need to finesse twice in diamonds, which will be possible only if you pay proper attention to the entry position.

Suppose you cash the king of clubs at trick two and continue with a finesse of the nine of clubs. If East produces the queen you will be short of an entry to dummy and will make the contract only if East has the kings of both spades and diamonds. The same applies if East shows out on the second round of clubs. You will have to give priority to establishing the clubs, and again you will be short of an entry for two diamond finesses.

The way to overcome the difficulty is to lead the seven of clubs for a finesse of the nine at trick two. If this loses to the queen, dummy will have the entries for two diamond finesses. If the club finesse succeeds, you can use the entry for a diamond finesse at trick three. If West produces the king of diamonds you will need to rely on a 3–2 club break. But if the diamond finesse succeeds, you can overtake the king of clubs with the ace and force out the queen. Dummy will eventually regain the lead with the ace of hearts to run the clubs and take a further diamond finesse.

This line of play loses when East has a singleton queen of clubs but gains in many other cases.

♠ A 7 5	
♡ A	*Match-point pairs*
◇ A Q J 8 3	*Game all*
♣ A Q 5 2	*Dealer North*

	N	S
♠ K J 4	1 ◇	1 ♡
♡ Q 10 9 8 6 4 3	3 ♣	3 ♡
◇ 7	3 ♠	3 NT
♣ 6 3		

West leads the nine of spades against your contract of three no trumps. How do you plan the play?

On the lead there are six top tricks, and it may be possible to develop three extra tricks in diamonds if the suit breaks favourably. But will nine tricks be enough to give you a good score? Your contract is a little eccentric, to put it kindly. It seems probable that most of the pairs in the field will play in four hearts, and it is clear that they will make at least ten tricks.

To have a chance of a decent score, therefore, you must live dangerously by playing on hearts, and you must take heed of the entry position before playing from dummy to the first trick. The ace of spades is the card to play in order to conserve entries in your own hand. After unblocking the ace of hearts, you can enter hand by taking the marked spade finesse. You must then hope to take the right view of the hearts. It is a fifty-fifty guess whether to continue with the ten of hearts or the queen. Most players will no doubt elect to play the queen, thinking it more fun to pin a doubleton knave than to drop a doubleton king.

If all goes smoothly you will end up with eleven or twelve tricks, depending on how accurately you read the ending. And if you misjudge the heart position? Well, a bottom is only a bottom.

Here is another hand with a similar theme.

♠ K 6
♡ 7 5 4
◇ A K 10 9 8 2   *Game all*
♣ A Q   *Dealer North*

	N	S
♠ A J 3	1 ◇	2 ♣
♡ A 10 2	3 ◇	3 NT
◇ 4		
♣ J 10 9 7 4 2		

West leads the four of spades against your contract of three no trumps. How do you plan the play?

You are naturally glad to have escaped a heart lead. It seems reasonable to win the first trick in hand, lead a club to the ace and continue with the queen of clubs. If the king appears you will have at least ten tricks. If the king of clubs is held up you can switch to diamonds, playing out the ace, king and ten in the hope of either dropping an honour card or finding a 3–3 break. This is a good line of play with a 78 per cent chance of success.

But why should you be content with 78 per cent when 100 per cent is available? The contract is unbeatable on the one assumption that West has led his fourth-best spade.

The correct play at trick one is the king of spades from dummy followed by the ace and queen of clubs. If the king of clubs is held up, cross to hand with the ace of spades and continue the club attack. The defenders are welcome to score three spade tricks and the king of clubs, for you will be sure of the remainder.

You cannot afford to play low from dummy on the first trick in case East produces the queen of spades. This would knock out one of your entries prematurely and compel you to adopt the inferior line of play.

♠ Q 5
♡ 7 4   *Match-point pairs*
◇ A K J 7 2   *Love all*
♣ 10 6 4 3   *Dealer South*

                             S   *N*
♠ J 10 9 4 3   1 ♠   2 ◇
♡ A K   2 NT   3 NT
◇ Q 8 3
♣ A J 9

West hits you in the weak spot with a lead of the queen of
hearts. How do you plan the play?

There is no time to develop the spades since the defenders
are a tempo ahead, but other declarers are likely to be faced
with exactly the same problem. The ninth trick will have to
come from clubs, which will be easy enough if the club
honours are divided or both with East. It might even be
possible to establish a tenth trick in clubs, but you would
need three entries to dummy, two to finesse in clubs and one
to cash the established winner.

You might gain the three entries you need by overtaking
the queen of diamonds at trick two. That would work well
enough on a 3–2 break, but the diamonds could be 4–1. It
would be unwise to put the contract in jeopardy for the
dubious chance of an overtrick.

What you can do to improve your prospects, however, is
to make a routine unblocking play by leading the eight of
diamonds to dummy's knave. If East should happen to drop
the nine or ten you have a free shot at the overtrick. After a
losing club finesse, you win the heart return and continue
with the queen of diamonds. If West follows suit you can
safely overtake in dummy. Then repeat the club finesse and
cash the ace, hoping for a 3–3 break. If East showed out on
the second round of diamonds, the way is clear to finesse the
seven of diamonds and cash your minor suit winners for ten
tricks and a top score.

♠ Q 5 4
♡ 10 9 3
◇ Q 10
♣ A K 9 5 2

N–S game
Dealer East

W	N	E	S
		1 ♠	Dbl

♠ A
♡ A J 8 5
◇ K 7 6 3
♣ J 10 6 4

W	N	E	S
2 ♠	3 ♠	—	3 NT
All pass			

The lead of the ten of spades runs to your ace. How do you plan the play?

Five clubs might have been easier, but your problem is to make nine tricks in no trumps. You need five tricks from the clubs, and the play for the drop gives a rather better chance than the first-round finesse. If you negotiate that hurdle you will have two chances of making the contract. West may have the knave of diamonds, or East may have both the king and queen of hearts. It will be possible to try for both chances in sequence, but only if you pay proper attention to the entry position.

This hand illustrates the value of a mental preview of the play before touching a card. Suppose you lead the knave of clubs to the king and continue with the ace, dropping the queen. You may return to hand with the ten of clubs and lead a diamond to the ten, but if this draws the ace and East returns a heart you will have no option but to let it run. Playing the ace of hearts would leave the diamonds blocked. You would have no way of enjoying two diamond tricks *and* the fifth club in dummy.

To avoid this blockage you must lead a diamond to the ten at trick two. The clubs can always wait. If the finesse of the ten of diamonds loses to the knave, you will still succeed in making the contract when East has both heart honours. He may play the king and another spade, but he will come under pressure on the run of the clubs and will be unable to keep four more winners.

A blocked suit usually spells trouble, especially when a vital entry is removed at an early stage.

♠ A 7 5 4
♡ J
◇ Q 10 8 3   *Game all*
♣ K 10 9 8   *Dealer South*

S	W	N	E
♠ J 3	1 ♣	1 ♡	3 ♣	—
♡ A Q 7	3 NT	*All pass*		
◇ K 5				
♣ A 7 5 4 3 2				

West leads the ten of hearts, and when dummy goes down you see that five clubs would have been easier once again. East plays the two of hearts under dummy's knave. How do you plan the play?

In a sense you have nine tricks, counting one spade, two hearts, and six clubs on a normal 2–1 break. The ace of diamonds is likely to be with West, however, and after un-blocking the clubs you will have no way back to your hand. The opponents may well be able to establish enough tricks to defeat you without leading a second heart.

There are in fact two equally sound methods of playing for nine tricks. The first is to lead the queen of diamonds from the table at trick two. In order to deny you a later diamond entry, West must either duck or take his ace and return the suit. With a diamond trick in the bag, you can afford to un-block the clubs by conceding a trick in the suit on the first or second round. The defenders will be able to score no more than three diamonds and one club.

But perhaps the simplest way of making the contract is to win the first trick with the queen of hearts and continue with the seven of hearts, discarding one of the blocking clubs from dummy. The other one goes on the ace of hearts, and the way is clear to run the club suit.

```
♠ A 10 9 3
♡ A 6
♢ A J 7 4              N–S game
♣ K Q 4               Dealer West
                 W      N      E      S
♠ K Q 8 5 4      1 ♡    Dbl    2 ♡    2 ♠
♡ 7 2            4 ♡    4 ♠    All pass
♢ 8 6 3
♣ 7 5 2
```

West leads the knave of hearts and East drops the king under dummy's ace. When you lead the ten of spades to your king West discards the three of hearts. A club lead is then won by dummy's queen, West playing the nine and East the three. How should you continue?

To have a chance of making the contract you need to find West with the king and queen of diamonds as well as the ace of clubs. This is not unlikely in view of the bidding and play to date. The trouble is that in order to develop the minor suits you need two further entries to hand and you do not have them. If you lead the three of spades from the table East will block the trumps by putting in the knave, and you will eventually find yourself stranded in dummy with no way of making more than nine tricks.

Something might be accomplished by enlisting the help of the defenders, however. The correct move is to exit in hearts at this point. If East wins the trick he will be unable to return a trump without giving you the two entries you need. A minor suit return will also solve the entry problem, while a further heart lead will give you a ruff and discard and an easy road to ten tricks.

If a diamond is returned you must allow West's king or queen to hold the trick, of course. This serves the dual purpose of gaining a tempo and guarding against a possible third-round ruff by East.

♠ 10 5 4
♡ Q 7 4
◇ K 7   *N–S game*
♣ A J 7 5 3   *Dealer South*

	S	W	N	E
♠ A K 9 7 6 3	1 ♠	Dbl	Rdbl	—
♡ J 5	3 ♠	—	4 ♠	*All pass*
◇ A 9 5 2				
♣ 9				

After cashing the ace and king of hearts, West leads the two of clubs to dummy's ace. How do you plan the play?

You expect to be able to discard one diamond loser on the queen of hearts and ruff the other in dummy. There should therefore be no problem unless the trumps break 4–0, in which case you might have to lose two trump tricks. A first-round trump finesse would guard against East holding all four trumps, but that is not a practical solution. You could not afford to lose to a singleton honour in the West hand and subsequently find East over-ruffing the third diamond.

The other way of dealing with four trumps in the East hand is by some sort of trump coup. This will involve reducing your trump holding to the same length as East's, and since entries to dummy are not too plentiful you had better start by ruffing a club at trick four. If you have any feeling for the value of small cards, however, you will not waste the three of spades, which may be needed at a later stage. The correct play is to unblock by ruffing a club with the six of spades. The play of the ace of spades will then expose the trump position.

If West shows out, you can lead a diamond to the king, discard a diamond on the queen of hearts, and ruff another club with the seven of spades. You continue by cashing the ace of diamonds and ruffing a diamond with the ten of spades. If East follows suit with a diamond, you can make sure of the contract by leading any card from dummy and playing your three of spades when the queen or knave of trumps appears. On the enforced trump return the marked finesse gives you ten tricks.

The point of preserving the three of trumps becomes apparent when East proves to have only two diamonds. After over-ruffing the ten of spades with his knave, East will be reduced to the queen and eight of trumps and one other card which is likely to be a heart. Once again a trump return enables you to score the rest of the tricks by taking the marked finesse. And on a heart return you are in the happy position of being able to ruff in hand with the three of spades and over-ruff in dummy with the five. Thus at the right time the lead is in the right place for you to pick up the outstanding trumps without loss.

The complete hand:

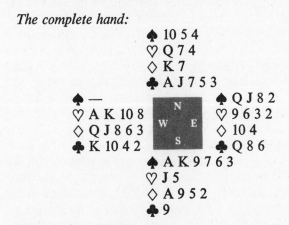

```
                  ♠ 10 5 4
                  ♡ Q 7 4
                  ◇ K 7
                  ♣ A J 7 5 3
  ♠ —                          ♠ Q J 8 2
  ♡ A K 10 8        N          ♡ 9 6 3 2
  ◇ Q J 8 6 3    W     E       ◇ 10 4
  ♣ K 10 4 2        S          ♣ Q 8 6
                  ♠ A K 9 7 6 3
                  ♡ J 5
                  ◇ A 9 5 2
                  ♣ 9
```

Play out the hand and see what will happen to any declarer who is not far-sighted enough to hang on to his three of trumps.

♠ 7 6 4 3
♡ J 10 9 6 2
◇ K 10 9   *Game all*
♣ A   *Dealer South*
                            S   N
♠ A Q   2 NT   3 ♡
♡ A Q   3 NT   —
◇ A Q 6 5
♣ K 10 5 3 2

The lead of the eight of clubs inconveniently removes an entry from dummy. At trick two you lead a small heart to your queen, which holds the trick. When you cash the ace of hearts, however, East discards the two of spades. How should you continue?

There are eight top tricks and chances of developing the ninth in any one of the four suits. It might be possible to set up a long club trick, for instance, but you might have to let East in twice and if the spade finesse lost you could lose too many tricks.

Four diamond tricks would see you home. If you had nothing better to play for you would no doubt tackle the diamonds by leading low to the king and running the ten on the way back. East is likely to have length in diamonds since he is short in hearts, but it would be annoying to lose to a doubleton knave in the West hand.

What about the heart suit as a source of extra tricks? Two entries to dummy will be needed in order to establish and cash the hearts, and they may be obtained by leading a small diamond for a finesse of the nine. If the finesse loses you can subsequently lead a small diamond to the ten, knock out the king of hearts, and re-enter dummy by overtaking the queen of diamonds with the king. Unfortunately, this plan suffers from the same defect as the play to establish clubs. If East scores a trick with the knave of diamonds he will return a spade, and you may then lose five tricks.

In view of the emphasis on placing the lead in the last chapter, it may occur to you that you need to find a way of losing the lead first to West, who can do no damage. This can be arranged by using dummy's entries in a different order. The sure method of making nine tricks is to lead the queen of diamonds at trick four and overtake with the king. Then return the knave of hearts and discard a club from hand.

The point is that if you can score four hearts you need only two tricks from the diamond suit. You can win the club return and lead a small diamond, thus creating a second entry in dummy. If East produces the knave of diamonds and leads a spade, you can even afford to try for an overtrick by taking the finesse.

There is one further trap. If West refuses to take the king of hearts, do not make the mistake of discarding another club on a fourth heart. That may lead to defeat if East is hanging on to five clubs. If you wish to startle the kibitzers you can discard the ace of diamonds on the fourth heart. But a more workmanlike approach is to abandon the hearts and run the ten of diamonds, thus retaining good chances of overtricks.

The full hand:

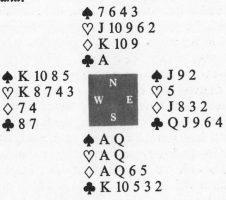

```
              ♠ 7 6 4 3
              ♡ J 10 9 6 2
              ◇ K 10 9
              ♣ A
♠ K 10 8 5                    ♠ J 9 2
♡ K 8 7 4 3        N          ♡ 5
◇ 7 4          W       E      ◇ J 8 3 2
♣ 8 7              S          ♣ Q J 9 6 4
              ♠ A Q
              ♡ A Q
              ◇ A Q 6 5
              ♣ K 10 5 3 2
```

♠ A K J 6 3
♡ A Q 4
◇ 9 6 2
♣ 10 7

Love all
Dealer North

N	S
1 ♠	2 ♣

♠ 5
♡ J 7 6
◇ A K 10 4
♣ Q J 9 8 3

N	S
2 ♠	2 NT
3 NT	—

West leads the two of hearts against your contract of three no trumps. How do you plan the play?

On the face of it nine tricks appear to be there, counting three clubs and two tricks in each of the other suits. The opening lead marks West with a four-card heart suit, and there is therefore no danger of losing more than two hearts.

The danger comes from a different quarter. If you play low from dummy on the first trick East may win and return not a heart but a diamond, attacking the entries needed for establishing your clubs. Whether you win the diamond switch or not, you may then make no more than seven tricks.

A case can be made for putting up the ace of hearts and leading a club at trick two, but this line of play is not proof against certain distributions of the cards. East may win the first club and lead a diamond, or West may win the first club and lead a spade, and in either case the defenders may establish five tricks before you can come to nine.

The correct card to play from dummy at trick one is neither the ace nor the four but the queen of hearts. If East produces the king, the knave of hearts becomes an extra entry in your hand and ensures that the clubs can be brought in. You will win the diamond switch and lead a club. If East wins the first club and leads another diamond you can afford to duck, and the defenders will be unable to score more than one heart, one diamond and two clubs.

♠ A J 10 4
♡ A 9
◇ A Q J 5   *N–S game*
♣ A 8 3   *Dealer North*

	N	S
♠ Q 8 7 6 2	2 NT	3 ♠
♡ J 4 3	4 ♣	4 ♠
◇ 10 3		
♣ 7 5 4		

Prospects do not look bright when West leads the king of clubs and dummy goes down. You allow West to hold the first trick but win the next lead of the queen of clubs with the ace. How should you continue?

There are no fewer than five potential losers and you must find a way of disposing of two of them. The big problem is the lack of a quick entry to your hand. You can eventually gain access in trumps, of course, but even if the diamond finesse is right you will still have to lose two clubs and a heart. The play of the ace and another trump will therefore succeed only when the king of spades is single.

It must be better to play for the spade finesse to be right, attempting to gain entry to your hand in diamonds. The correct play at trick three is the queen of diamonds from the table. If an opponent wins this trick you will have in the ten of diamonds the entry you need to take the trump finesse. The lead of the queen of spades will cater for three trumps in the West hand. When the trump finesse succeeds you will be able to discard your losing hearts on dummy's diamonds and claim ten tricks.

If the queen of diamonds is allowed to win at trick three, continue with the ace of diamonds and a diamond ruff. In the absence of an over-ruff you will again score ten tricks when the trump finesse is right.

This deal comes from a friendly match between Scotland

and Iceland in 1969. Tom Culbertson earned a swing for Scotland by finding the play to make four spades.

♠ 9 5 2
♡ 6 2
◇ Q 5   *Love all*
♣ A K Q 8 7 3   *Dealer West*

	W	N	E	S
♠ A J 10	1 ♠	2 ♣	—	3 NT
♡ A K J 4	*All pass*			
◇ J 10 9 7 4				
♣ 2				

West leads the four of spades, East plays the queen and you win with the ace. The position of the remaining high cards is marked by the bidding. From the lead you know that West started with no more than five spades, but you dare not tackle the diamonds for fear that West will establish five tricks before you can make nine. You therefore hope for a 3–3 club break, leading a club to the ace and discarding the four of hearts on the king of clubs. On these two tricks East follows suit with the five and the six and West with the four and the ten. How should you continue?

The even club break is still possible, but in order to guard against the risk of a 4–2 break you must discard the ten of spades on the queen of clubs. If West is unable to follow suit he will also be embarrassed for a discard. He cannot afford to part with a spade, for that would allow you to play on diamonds with impunity. West must therefore throw a red card, and you can then continue with a fourth club, discarding the knave of spades from your hand.

The effect of the unblocking discards is to create a potential entry for the long clubs in the nine of spades, thus preventing the enemy from pressing home the spade attack. West can spare a spade on the fourth club, of course, and East will probably switch to a heart. You will win with the ace and lead a diamond for West to win.

At this point West will try to make a nuisance of himself by cashing the king of spades, but you can discard a diamond secure in the knowledge that either the queen of hearts will drop or West will have to lead a heart into your tenace. Let us have a look at the full hand.

♠ 9 5 2
♡ 6 2
◇ Q 5
♣ A K Q 8 7 3

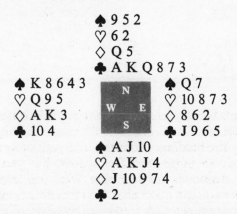

♠ K 8 6 4 3
♡ Q 9 5
◇ A K 3
♣ 10 4

♠ Q 7
♡ 10 8 7 3
◇ 8 6 2
♣ J 9 6 5

♠ A J 10
♡ A K J 4
◇ J 10 9 7 4
♣ 2

As you can see, the defenders are helpless once you have discarded the blocking spades.

8. Killing an Entry

When you have learned to look after your entries you will still be no more than part of the way towards solving all your problems of communication. In a large group of hands success depends not on preserving your own entries but on preventing the defenders from making the best use of theirs. These are the hands on which you cannot afford to get on with the normal business of drawing trumps and establishing your tricks. Something leads you to suspect that the defenders will find a way of defeating the contract if you ignore their activities. In such cases priority must be given to the task of spiking the enemy guns. Only when that objective has been achieved can you start counting winners instead of losers.

Recognition of the hazard is half the battle. If you are to take effective counter-measures you must first see where the danger lies. The threat may be that of an enemy ruff, or perhaps a trump promotion, and the remedy may be to transfer a loser from one suit to another. Alternatively, you may be threatened by an impending force which can be overcome only by attacking the enemy entries in the right order. A dangerous defender can often be rendered harmless by removing his entry at an early stage, before he has established a winner. On other hands it may be necessary to sever communications in a particular suit in order to prepare the ground for a throw-in play.

The declarer enjoys an advantage in that he exercises a measure of control over the timing of the defensive entries.

One of the simplest ways of putting the defenders out of touch with each other is the hold-up play. By refusing to part with his stopper until one defender is exhausted of the suit, the declarer may prevent the threat from developing. Hold-up play will be familiar to most readers, however, and in this chapter we shall examine other ways of killing entries.

Try your hand at this four-spade contract.

♠ A 7 4
♡ K J 6 3
◇ K 10 4   *N–S game*
♣ K 10 7   *Dealer South*

                           S   N
♠ Q J 9 8 5 2   1 ♠   3 NT
♡ 7   4 ♠   —
◇ 3
♣ A Q J 6 4

West leads the ten of hearts, you cover with the knave and the queen takes the trick. East switches to the eight of clubs. How do you plan the play?

On the face of it there are only three likely losers, a heart, a diamond and a spade, but this club switch looks ominous. East appears to be angling for a club ruff, and the danger is that he may have three spades headed by the king. In that case the play of the ace and another spade will not be good enough. On winning with the king East may be able to lead a diamond to his partner's ace and score a club ruff as the setting trick.

The solution to the problem, simple once you think of it, is to keep West off lead by exchanging your diamond loser for a heart loser. You should win the club in dummy and play the king of hearts, discarding your diamond when East produces the ace. Ruff the red suit return and play the ace and another spade, and the defenders will have no way of obtaining a club ruff.

This is an example of the Scissors Coup, so called because

its effect is to cut the defenders' lines of communication. It is in fact a loser-on-loser play that places the lead in the safe hand.

```
♠ 10 9 7 5 4
♡ 6                    Game all
♦ A K Q 8              Dealer South
♣ K Q 3                S          N
                       1 ♠        3 ♦
♠ A K J 6 2            3 ♡        3 ♠
♡ Q J 9 7              4 ♠        —
♦ 10 9 5
♣ 2
```

West leads the knave of clubs and dummy's king falls to the ace. On the club return you discard a heart from hand and capture the ten with the queen. When you lead a trump to your ace West discards the two of diamonds. How should you continue?

Eleven tricks appear to be a matter of routine on this hand. When dummy regains the lead you will be able to pick up the trumps by taking the marked finesse, thus losing only a club and a heart. When the contract looks particularly easy, however, it is always as well to ask yourself what could go wrong.

The answer is that East may be void in diamonds. In that case, if you lead a diamond at trick four, East will ruff, put his partner in with a heart, and score a second diamond ruff to put the contract one down.

This hand is a good test of awareness at the bridge table. There is no reason to suspect such a diabolical diamond break, but it costs nothing to guard against it. A heart trick has to be lost in any case, and the right time to lose it is at trick four. The heart lead puts the defenders out of touch with each other and guarantees ten tricks without reducing the chances of making eleven.

♠ Q 10 8 4 3
♡ Q 7 5 2   *Game all*
◊ J 4   *Dealer South*
♣ 6 2   S   N
                     2 ♣   2 ◊
♠ A   2 ♡   4 ♡
♡ A K J 10 8   6 ♡   —
◊ A K 6
♣ A 10 7 3

West leads the three of hearts, which looks like a good
start for the defence when dummy goes down. You play low
from the table, East discards the two of diamonds, and your
eight of hearts wins the first trick. How should you continue?

There are just four top tricks in the side suits and no
prospects of developing a fifth. Eight tricks are therefore
required from trumps, which means that you must score
them all separately. In theory it should be possible to ruff a
diamond and two clubs in dummy, but in practice there is a
difficulty. If you concede a club trick in the process of
preparing your cross-ruff, West is likely to be able to win and
lead a second trump, which will leave you a trick short.

This would have been an easy hand on any lead but a
trump. Is there any way of preventing the defenders from
drawing a second round of trumps?

At least you know that East has no trump to lead. If you
cannot keep West off lead in clubs you may have better luck
in diamonds. There is no certainty of success, but you can
give yourself a good chance by leading the six of diamonds
from hand at trick two. If East has the queen of diamonds
and West at least three cards in the suit you are home. After
winning the return you will cash the ace and king of diamonds, discarding the losing club from dummy, and cross-
ruff the remainder for twelve tricks.

The next hand is a little more complex.

♠ 9				
♡ 7 3				
◇ 10 8 7 6 4 3 2		*E–W game*		
♣ Q 9 4		*Dealer West*		
	W	*N*	*E*	*S*
♠ K Q J 6 5 4 2	1 ♣	—	3 ♣	4 ♠
♡ A K Q J	Dbl	*All pass*		
◇ 9				
♣ 5				

West leads the ace of diamonds, and the sight of dummy brings you little joy. East drops the king of diamonds on the first trick, and West continues with the five of diamonds to his partner's knave. After ruffing, how should you continue?

The contract is not completely hopeless, although you could wish for better intermediates in trumps. West is likely to have the ace of spades for his double, and you must hope that he does not have four trumps. But the situation is loaded with danger even if the trumps are 3–2. Do you see what will happen if you lead the king of spades at this point? West will win and lead a club to put his partner on lead, and the diamond return will promote a second trump trick for the defence.

On this hand it hardly seems possible to keep East off lead. East has only one diamond left, however, and if you could reach the table you could achieve a scissors coup of a sort by leading a diamond yourself and ditching your losing club. This would take the sting out of the diamond situation and avert the threat of a trump promotion.

The obvious way to reach the table is by ruffing the third round of hearts, relying on a 4–3 break in the suit. But if you look more deeply into the position you may realize that this line of play is about as safe as going over Niagara in a leaky barrel. The trouble is that if East has a fourth heart he will be able to give his partner a heart ruff after winning his diamond trick. Come to think of it, there is danger even when West has the fourth heart, for there is nothing to stop West from ruffing his partner's queen of diamonds. A heart return would then enable East to score the setting trick with a ruff. It would therefore appear that it cannot be right to ruff the third heart in dummy no matter how the suit is distributed.

If the defender with four hearts also has the ten of spades, however, you may succeed by ruffing the *fourth* heart on the table. When there is no over-ruff you can proceed as planned by discarding your losing club on a diamond.

This is the only line of play that offers a real chance of making the contract. The sort of distribution that you have to play for is shown in the full diagram below.

```
                    ♠ 9
                    ♡ 7 3
                    ◇ 10 8 7 6 4 3 2
                    ♣ Q 9 4
  ♠ A 10 7                        ♠ 8 3
  ♡ 10 8 5 2          N           ♡ 9 6 4
  ◇ A 5          W         E      ◇ K Q J
  ♣ K J 8 3           S           ♣ A 10 7 6 2
                    ♠ K Q J 6 5 4 2
                    ♡ A K Q J
                    ◇ 9
                    ♣ 5
```

Obviously there is a possibility of going two down, but the risk seems well worth taking.

A different method of putting an entry to sleep is illustrated in the next hand.

♠ 5
♡ K 10 6 5 3
◇ K 7 6 2   *E–W game*
♣ K J 2   *Dealer North*

          W   *N*   *E*   *S*

♠ A Q J 8 7 4 2   —   —   4 ♠
♡ 7   *All pass*
◇ Q J
♣ Q 10 9

Your pre-emptive bid of four spades is passed out and
West leads the nine of diamonds. When dummy goes down
you are pleasantly surprised to see that you actually have a
play for the contract. How do you set about it?

You must hope for a lucky trump position, of course. With
a loser in each of the side suits, you cannot afford a trump
loser, which means that you will need to find East with the
doubleton king.

There is cause for concern in the diamond situation, since
the lead of the nine suggests shortage. Nothing can be done
to avert defeat if the nine is a singleton, but suppose West has
a doubleton diamond. If you play low from dummy East
will no doubt hold up his ace in order to maintain communication with his partner. When you attempt to enter dummy
in clubs, the opponents will take the aces of clubs, hearts and
diamonds, and a further diamond lead will promote the
setting trick in trumps.

To give yourself a chance when the diamonds are 5–2 you
must attack the ace of diamonds by playing the king from
dummy at trick one. This will create an insoluble dilemma
for East if he has no outside entry. If he ducks, he permits
you to draw trumps straight away, while if he takes his ace
he surrenders the chance of promoting a trump trick for his
partner.

♠ K 6   *Match-point pairs*
♡ Q 8 4 3   *Love all*
◇ A J 9 4   *Dealer East*
♣ 10 6 2   W   N   E   S
                                          1 ♡   1 ♠
♠ Q J 10 9 4 2   2 ◇   2 ♠   3 ♣   —
♡ 9 6   3 ◇   —   —   3 ♠
◇ 6   Dbl   *All pass*
♣ A J 9 5

West leads the seven of clubs, East plays the queen and you win with the ace. The king of spades wins the next trick, and East discards the seven of hearts on the second spade. West takes his ace and switches to the two of hearts. How do you plan the play?

Clearly you are not going to make this contract, for you have to lose a spade, two hearts, a club and a club ruff. Minus 100 should be a reasonable score, since the opponents would have chalked up 110 in three diamonds. What you must avoid at all costs is losing 300 by going two down.

What do you make of this two of hearts from West? If it is a singleton you have nothing to worry about. It can hardly be from three cards or the bidding of the opponents does not make sense. There is a danger, however, that West may have led the two from a holding of king doubleton. In that case, if you play low from dummy, East will win with the ten, cash the king of clubs and lead another club for his partner to ruff. He will then be in a position to overtake the king of hearts with his ace and give his partner another club ruff to put you two down.

To guard against this possibility you must block the hearts by playing the queen from the table. East is thus denied a second entry in the suit and the defenders are limited to one club ruff.

Second-hand-high play to prevent an entry finesse is perhaps more familiar as a defensive manœuvre.

♠ 9 6 5 4 3
♡ K 6 5 3
◇ 7   *Game all*
♣ K Q 6   *Dealer West*

	W	N	E	S

♠ A K 2   —   —   1 ◇   1 ♡
♡ J 10 9 8 4 2   3 ♣   4 ♡ *All pass*
◇ 10 5 4
♣ 7

West leads the eight of spades and you see that you have
landed in a highly optimistic game. East plays the ten of
spades and you win the first trick with the ace. How should
you continue?

There is a loser in every suit, and the situation must be
hopeless if the spades are 4–1. On a 3–2 spade break you will
have a chance of parking the spade loser on one of dummy's
clubs. It is tempting to lead a club at trick two, but this can
succeed only if West ducks. He is more likely to take his ace
and lead a second spade, leaving you with no quick way of
reaching dummy to take your discard. Before you can do so
East will gain the lead in diamonds and cash his spade to put
you one down.

If you are to avoid a spade loser on this hand you must give
priority to cutting the enemy communications. East may have
no entry in hearts or clubs but he will certainly have one in
diamonds. You should therefore lead a diamond at trick two.

If diamonds are continued you can ruff in dummy and lead
the king of clubs, while if a spade is returned you can win and
lead a trump from hand. If the aces of clubs and hearts are
with West, as you hope, East will be unable to gain the lead
again and your losing spade will eventually be discarded on
a club.

♠ A 8 5
♡ A K 6 4
◇ 9 4   *Love all*
♣ A 10 6 2   *Dealer East*

	W	N	E	S
♠ Q 10 9 6 3			1 ♡	1 ♠
♡ 7 3	—	4 ♠	*All pass*	
◇ K Q J				
♣ Q 8 4				

West leads the knave of hearts to dummy's ace. When you cash the ace of spades East drops the king. How should you continue?

The king of clubs is marked in the East hand by the opening bid, so your only losers would appear to be a spade, a diamond and a club. However, in order to develop your tricks you have to lose the lead several times, and there is a danger that your trumps may be exhausted by heart leads.

Suppose you concede a trick to the knave of spades immediately. You can win the heart return, draw trumps, and lead the king of diamonds. But when East takes his ace he will lead another heart to force out your last trump, and you will never be able to enjoy a second club trick.

Clearly you must control the timing of the enemy entries better, making sure that West is not offered his trump trick until he has no heart left to return. The correct move at trick three is to attack diamonds and knock out the ace. Win the heart return in dummy and continue with a low club towards your queen. East will do best to take his king and lead a third heart, but you can counter by ruffing with the nine of spades. Whether West over-ruffs or not, you will then have no difficulty in making your contract.

♠ A K J 10 3
♡ A K 9 5 3   *Love all*
◊ 2   *Dealer West*
♣ K 4   W   N   E   S
                      1 ◊   Dbl   3 ◊   —
♠ 9 7 5 2   —   Dbl   —   3 ♠
♡ 7 4   —   4 ♠   *All pass*
◊ 10 9 6
♣ J 5 3 2

The game has its compensations for the poor card-holder.
West leads the ten of hearts and East plays the six under the
ace. When you cash the ace of spades East plays the six and
West the four. How should you continue?

The ace of clubs is likely to be well placed, so the problem
is to find a way of restricting the major suit losers to one
trick. This should be possible provided that the hearts break
no worse than 4–2.

It would not be safe to cash the king of spades at this stage,
however. If East has four hearts West is likely to have three
trumps, and he will not be so helpful as to over-ruff when you
ruff the third round of hearts. He will discard, and you will
be stuck in hand with no quick way back to dummy. Whether
you lead a club or a diamond, West will win and cash the
queen of trumps, drawing your last trump and leaving you
with at least one loser in every suit.

Should you then cash the king of hearts at trick three and
continue with a heart ruff? That is no better. West might
over-ruff, put his partner in with a diamond, and over-ruff
another heart to put you one down.

First you must sever communications by leading a diamond. The way will then be clear for you to ruff hearts
without suffering more than one over-ruff.

♠ A K 8 2
♡ J 9 8 5 4
◇ A K   *E–W game*
♣ 10 3   *Dealer South*

	S	N
♠ 7 3	3 ♣	3 ♡
♡ 3	4 ♣	5 ♣
◇ 8 6 4		
♣ A Q J 8 7 5 2		

West leads the knave of spades to dummy's ace. How do you plan the play?

Prospects seem good if the trumps are no worse than 3–1. The trump finesse offers a fifty-fifty chance, but better odds can be obtained by ruffing the losing diamond in dummy. A straightforward method of play would be to cash the ace and king of diamonds, lead the three of clubs to your ace and ruff the third diamond with the ten of clubs. There could be a problem about returning to hand, however. It would be too risky to attempt a third-round spade ruff, and you would therefore have to lead a heart.

Conceding a trick to the defence at this point has dangers of its own. West might have started with only three cards in diamonds and three clubs including the king and the nine, in which case a further diamond lead from East would promote a second defensive trump trick.

The danger is easily averted by the exercise of a little forethought. The correct play is to concede the heart at trick four, after cashing the ace and king of diamonds. At this early stage the opponents are much less likely to be able to inflict any damage. You can win the trump return with the ace, ruff the diamond in dummy, and cash the king of spades as an extra precaution. After a heart ruff you can lead the queen of clubs to knock out the king. Since there will be a clear path back to your hand, the defenders will then be unable to develop a trump promotion.

♠ 9 6 3
♡ A 9 6 5   *Love all*
◊ 7 6 4   *Dealer West*
♣ K 9 3   W   N   E   S
                    2 ♡*   —   —   2 NT
♠ Q 8 2   —   3 NT   *All pass*
♡ Q 4 3
◊ A K J 10 9
♣ A 4
                    * *Weak two bid, 6–10 points*

The opening lead is the ten of clubs. When you allow this
to hold the trick West continues with the seven of clubs to
your ace, East echoing with the eight and the six. You cash
the ace and king of diamonds, and to your relief East drops
the queen on the second round. How should you continue?

The weak two bid marks West with all six hearts. He is
also known to have two clubs and three diamonds, and must
therefore have two spades including one of the top honours
to make up his quota of points. Clearly a throw-in play is the
best bet to produce the ninth trick. One idea that may occur
to you is to cash one more diamond and then lead the three
of hearts, intending to duck in dummy when West plays the
ten. West would then have to give you the ninth trick either
in hearts or in spades.

But West is not bound to co-operate in this plan. He may
frustrate you by playing the two of hearts under your three,
forcing dummy to win the trick and cutting you off for ever
from your remaining diamond winners.

The throw-in has to be managed in a different way. You
must hope that West's spades are either the ace and another
or the king and the knave. In either case East will have no
more than one entry in the suit and you will be able to break
contact between the defenders. The correct play is a low
spade from hand at trick five.

If East wins the trick, West will eventually be end-played

in hearts whether he discards the ace of spades on the third club or not. West may avoid the end-play by playing the ace of spades on the first round and exiting with his third diamond, but you will then be able to establish the queen of spades as your ninth trick.

The full hand:

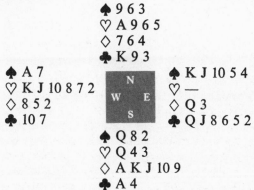

```
                    ♠ 9 6 3
                    ♡ A 9 6 5
                    ◇ 7 6 4
                    ♣ K 9 3
    ♠ A 7                           ♠ K J 10 5 4
    ♡ K J 10 8 7 2                  ♡ —
    ◇ 8 5 2                         ◇ Q 3
    ♣ 10 7                          ♣ Q J 8 6 5 2
                    ♠ Q 8 2
                    ♡ Q 4 3
                    ◇ A K J 10 9
                    ♣ A 4
```

Note that the contract cannot be made if you run the entire diamond suit at once, for this involves weakening dummy in some vital respect.

9. Removing an Exit Card

Although we have dealt with problems of communication in the last three chapters, we have not quite finished with the subject. The control of enemy exit cards is an aspect of communication play that is worthy of separate study.

This is mainly an exercise in hypothetical reasoning. The problem arises on a familiar type of hand where the contract is in danger only if a particular situation obtains—a key honour offside combined with an enemy ruff or a bad break in a side suit, for instance. In such cases it may take a far-sighted appraisal of the situation to avoid disaster.

On these hands you are concerned neither with destroying the enemy entries nor with securing your own. The idea is to reduce the options open to a defender by removing some of his exit cards, thus ensuring that if he gains the lead in a dangerous situation he will be unable to make an embarrassing return. The object of the exercise may be to prepare a safe way back to your hand on any return that the defender may make. More often it will be to compel the defender to open up a new suit to your advantage.

In the latter case it is evident that the removal of exit cards has much in common with elimination play. The situations that we shall study can hardly be classed as full eliminations, but many take the form of semi-eliminations executed at an early stage in the play. The main difficulty lies in recognizing the problem in time.

Experienced players are likely to do the right thing in the first example where the danger is glaringly obvious.

♠ A J 4
♡ A J 10 3
◇ K 7 5   *Love all*
♣ 7 3 2   *Dealer West*

	W	N	E	S
♠ Q 10 9 6 2	1 ♣	—	—	1 ♠
♡ K 7 5	2 ♣	3 ♠	All pass	
◇ Q 8 4				
♣ K J				

West leads the queen of hearts and you win in hand with the king. How should you continue?

Although there are four potential losers in the minor suits you can expect to discard one of them on the fourth heart. In a contract of four spades you would have no option but to try the trump finesse. In three spades you can afford the loss of a trump trick and should play for maximum safety.

The queen of hearts is almost certainly a singleton, and it is not impossible for East to have the king of spades. The danger is that a losing trump finesse will result in West obtaining a heart ruff. That will not matter if West has only two trumps, for he will then have to open up one of the minor suits to your advantage. But if West has three trumps he will be able to exit safely in trumps after ruffing the heart. You may then be unable to avoid the loss of three further tricks in the minor suits.

All risk can be avoided by leading a trump to the ace at trick two and continuing with the knave of trumps. If East is able to win he may give his partner a heart ruff, but West will have to allow you to score two tricks in the minor suits on his return. This line of play ensures the contract on any lie of the cards that is consistent with the bidding.

The next example introduces a slight complication.

♠ A 8
♡ A Q 6 3
◇ J 7 2   *Game all*
♣ K 4 3 2   *Dealer South*

	S	N
♠ K 3	1 NT	2 ♣
♡ J 10 7 2	2 ♡	4 ♡
◇ A 10 5		
♣ A Q 10 7		

West leads the five of clubs and you capture the knave with your ace. How should you continue?

Three no trumps would have been an easy contract, whereas in four hearts your task is complicated by the mirror distribution in the two hands. On a normal 3–2 trump break, however, the chance of success must be very high. You can afford to lose a trump and two diamonds and still make the contract. What you cannot afford is to lose a club ruff as well, and that is a distinct possibility on the lead.

Clearly the play of the ace and another heart is superior to the finesse, for this cuts down the risk of West obtaining a club ruff. But if East has the doubleton king of trumps he may still be able to give his partner a ruff. West will then exit comfortably with a spade, and you may yet go down if you run into an unfavourable diamond situation.

It is not good enough, therefore, to play the ace and another heart immediately. First you must remove West's safe exit in spades by cashing the ace and the king. In the dangerous case where West has three small trumps and a singleton club he will then find himself without a good return after ruffing the club. A spade lead will concede a ruff and discard, while a diamond return will give you two tricks in the suit.

♠ Q 10 8 4 3
♡ A 4 2
◇ 5   *E–W game*
♣ A 7 3 2   *Dealer South*

                          S   N
♠ K J 9 5   1 NT   2 ♣
♡ K 9   2 ♠   4 ♠
◇ K 8 3
♣ K 10 6 5

West leads the nine of clubs, East puts in the knave, and you win with the king. How should you proceed?

At first glance there appear to be no more than three losers—a spade, a diamond and a club. But once again the lead looks suspiciously like a singleton, and there is some danger of losing a club ruff as well. If you lead a spade at trick two, for instance, East may win and lead a club for his partner to ruff. West will be able to exit safely in hearts, and your contract will be dependent on the position of the ace of diamonds.

The answer to this type of problem usually becomes clear when you review the likely course of the play in your mind. Once you think about West's exit in hearts you are half way towards planning to remove it. The logical play is to eliminate the hearts by ruffing the third round before touching trumps. This gives you an extra chance when the trumps are 2–2. If East wins the ace of spades and gives his partner a club ruff, West may now have no safe return. Lacking a third spade, he will have to lead a diamond, providing you with a club discard in dummy, or concede a ruff and discard by returning a heart.

Naturally if East returns a diamond after winning the ace of spades, you must cover his card in order to place the lead firmly in the West hand and avoid the risk of a club ruff.

On the next hand the threat is that of a trump promotion instead of a ruff.

♠ A J 9
♡ 7 6 3
◇ A K 9 5 3
♣ Q 7

	W	N	E	S
	1 NT (12–14)	Dbl	—	2 NT

♠ Q 10 4
♡ A Q J 8 5
◇ 8 2
♣ 10 6 3

	W	N	E	S
	—	3 ◇	—	3 ♡
	—	4 ♡	All pass	

N–S game
Dealer West

West starts with the ace and king of clubs, on which his partner plays the four and five. You ruff the third club in dummy while East follows suit with the knave. How should you continue?

The contract is doomed if the spade finesse is wrong, for on the bidding East cannot have both major suit kings. It is quite possible for West to have both kings, however, and that makes the trump finesse too risky. If West wins and leads a fourth club, his partner may be able to uppercut with the nine or ten of hearts, thus establishing a second trump trick for the defence.

You can avoid this danger by leading a trump to the ace and continuing with the queen, but if you are looking ahead you may spot a further snag. If West has three trumps headed by the king and only two diamonds he will return a diamond, and you will be unable to return to hand without conceding a spade trick or an over-ruff.

For optimum safety, therefore, you must remove the exit cards in diamonds. The correct play is a heart to the ace followed by the ace and king of diamonds and another heart from the table. On the assumption that the spade finesse is right, no return from either defender can then hurt you.

♠ Q 8
♡ A 10 5 3
◇ A K 9 5 4
♣ A K

Game all
Dealer West

	W	N	E	S
	1 ♣	Dbl	—	1 ♡
	—	3 ♡	—	4 ♡
	All pass			

♠ J 9 4
♡ K 8 7 6 2
◇ Q 6 2
♣ 9 4

West attacks with the ace, king and another spade. You discard a diamond from the table and win the third trick in hand. How should you continue?

The contract is safe provided that you do not lose two trump tricks. There is nothing to be done if East has all four trumps, but you can guard against four trumps in the West hand by playing the king on the first round. Looking deeper into the position you may see a further complication. If you play the king of hearts at trick four and East shows out, you can be sure that West will split his honours on the second round. You may leave him in possession of the trick, win the club return in dummy, and cross to hand with the queen of diamonds to take a further trump finesse. But if West is void in diamonds he will score a ruff to put you one down. This is not such a far-fetched possibility. If West has four hearts he is sure to be short in diamonds and may well have none.

What about leading a heart to the ten at trick four, retaining the king as a subsequent entry? This is still not completely safe, for East may win and give his partner a diamond ruff.

The correct way to play the hand is to cash the ace and king of clubs and then return a heart to the king. If East shows out, let West hold the trick when he splits his honours on the next round and he will have no means of locking you in dummy.

♠ A Q 3
♡ K J 5 2
◇ A 8 7 2   *Love all*
♣ 8 3   *Dealer East*

	W	N	E	S
			1 ♣	1 ♡

♠ 9 5
♡ A 9 8 4 3   —   4 ♡   *All pass*
◇ K 6 4
♣ K 7 2

West leads the ten of clubs to his partner's ace, and East returns the queen of clubs which you win with the king. West follows to a third club, so you ruff low in dummy and return a small trump to your ace, East following with the six and West with the seven. How do you continue?

The odds favour the play for the drop in trumps rather than the finesse, but there is very little in it. There is some danger of losing a trick in each suit, since the spade finesse is sure to be wrong. If the diamonds break 3–3, however, you will be able to establish the fourth diamond for a spade discard. Can you see anything else that is worth trying?

In fact you can increase your chances considerably by leading a diamond to the ace, a diamond back to the king, and then taking the heart finesse. If East is able to win with the queen he may have no diamonds left, in which case he will either have to lead away from his king of spades or give you a ruff and discard. On this line of play you will make certain of your contract whenever East has one or two hearts and no more than three diamonds.

No risk is involved in the attempt to remove the exit cards in diamonds. East can hardly have five cards in the suit since he is known to have no more than five clubs.

The 'safety finesse' in trumps is a manœuvre that is often overlooked. Here is another example.

♠ K 10 5 2
♡ A 6
◇ K 10 7   *Game all*
♣ A K J 3   *Dealer North*

	N	S
♠ A J 9 8 3	1 ♣	1 ♠
♡ 10 7 4	3 ♠	4 ♠
◇ Q 5 4 2		
♣ 5		

West leads the two of hearts against your contract of four spades. How do you plan the play?

It would take more than a normal slice of bad luck to defeat this contract. You would have to misguess the trumps, fail to bring down the queen of clubs in three rounds, and then find the knave of diamonds offside. Such a chain of misfortune is not unknown, however, and you should look for a way of minimizing the danger before playing to the first trick.

Again you have the awkward nine-card trump holding that presents a difficult choice between the finesse and the drop. But in this case you can practically guarantee success when West has either two or three trumps. The first step must be to eliminate the hearts, and to that end you should allow East to win the first trick. On winning the heart return, you can enter hand with the ace of spades, ruff the third heart in dummy, cash the ace of clubs and ruff the three of clubs in your hand. Then lead a trump and insert the ten if West follows with a low card.

If East is able to win this trick he will be end-played, compelled to yield the tenth trick whether he returns a heart, a diamond or a club.

♠ Q 8 3 2
♡ 4 3 2
◇ J 7 6
♣ A K 2

N–S game
Dealer North

W	N	E	S
	—	3 ♡	3 ♠

♠ A 10 9 7 6 4
♡ A Q 5
◇ Q
♣ Q 8 3

W	N	E	S
—	4 ♠	—	—
Dbl	*All pass*		

To your mild surprise, West produces the knave of hearts as his opening lead. East contributes the ten and you win the trick with the queen. When you cash the ace of spades East discards the nine of diamonds, which surprises you not at all. How should you continue?

West must be a bit of an optimist to have doubled, although no doubt it was a blow to him to see the queen of spades in dummy. You may be able to punish his impertinence, for you are very close to making the doubled contract. You can afford the loss of a trump, a heart and a diamond, but there is a serious danger of losing a ruff as well.

East appears to have pre-empted on a six-card heart suit headed by the king, and it looks as though he has an entry card in diamonds to judge from his discard of the nine. Consider how the play is likely to develop if you lead a second spade at this point. West will win the trick with the king, put his partner in with a diamond lead, and ruff away your ace of hearts on the return. He will then get off lead with a club, and you will be left with an unavoidable fourth loser in hearts.

The solution, as you have probably realized, is to remove those comfortable exit cards from the West hand. Play three rounds of clubs, ending in your own hand, before leading a second trump. West is welcome to win the trick with his king, put his partner in with a diamond and ruff out your ace of hearts, for he will then find himself end-played. On the bidding East can hardly have both top diamonds, so West will be unable to lead a second diamond without creating a trick for dummy's knave. A club return, of course, will allow you to ruff in dummy and discard the losing heart from your hand.

Here is the full deal.

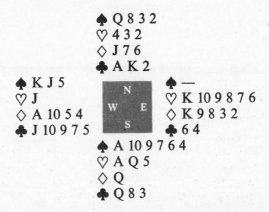

```
                    ♠ Q 8 3 2
                    ♡ 4 3 2
                    ◇ J 7 6
                    ♣ A K 2
    ♠ K J 5                          ♠ —
    ♡ J                              ♡ K 10 9 8 7 6
    ◇ A 10 5 4                       ◇ K 9 8 3 2
    ♣ J 10 9 7 5                     ♣ 6 4
                    ♠ A 10 9 7 6 4
                    ♡ A Q 5
                    ◇ Q
                    ♣ Q 8 3
```

This is a hand from the Far Eastern Championships of 1973. The declarer in four spades doubled was Patrick Huang of Taiwan, who read the position exactly and made the contract by cashing three rounds of clubs before leading a second spade.

Experts are not always so far-sighted, however. The next hand comes from a semi-final match of the 1974 Vanderbilt Cup, one of the major team events in the U.S.A. The contract was the same at both tables, and neither declarer found the play to give himself the best chance.

```
♠ 6 2                      E-W game
♡ Q 10 8 7 5              Dealer West
◇ Q 10 7 4         W      N      E       S
♣ A 7              —      —      2 ♠*    3 ♡
                   —      3 ♠    Dbl     Rdbl
♠ A 9 5            —      4 ♣    —       4 ♡
♡ A K J 9 2        All pass
◇ K 6 2
♣ 10 5
```

*   * Weak two bid, 6–10 points*

West leads the king of clubs to dummy's ace. You clear
the trumps with the ace and queen, East discarding a spade on
the second round. How should you continue?

The chance of losing only one diamond trick will be
brightest if you can persuade the opponents to open up the
suit for you. If you concede the club at this point West will
be able to switch to spades, and you will have to tackle
diamonds yourself. The correct play is the ace and another
spade in order to remove West's exit cards. East is marked
with six spades, which leaves West with only two. After
winning his club trick, therefore, West will have to lead a
diamond or concede a ruff and discard.

The full hand:

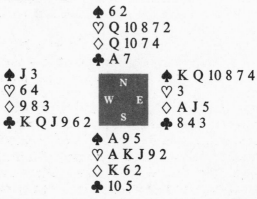

```
                    ♠ 6 2
                    ♡ Q 10 8 7 2
                    ◇ Q 10 7 4
                    ♣ A 7
    ♠ J 3                          ♠ K Q 10 8 7 4
    ♡ 6 4            N              ♡ 3
    ◇ 9 8 3       W     E           ◇ A J 5
    ♣ K Q J 9 6 2     S            ♣ 8 4 3
                    ♠ A 9 5
                    ♡ A K J 9 2
                    ◇ K 6 2
                    ♣ 10 5
```

Only West can win the club trick, and the diamond spots are such that he cannot lead the suit without allowing you to make two diamond tricks.

♠ 7 6			
♡ A 8 2		*N–S game*	
◇ K J 8 4 2		*Dealer South*	
♣ 9 8 3	*S*	*W*	*N*	*E*

	S	*W*	*N*	*E*
	1 ♡	1 ♠	2 ♡	—
♠ A J 8 5	3 ◇	—	4 ◇	—
♡ Q 10 9 4 3	4 ♡	*All pass*		
◇ A 9 6				
♣ A				

West leads the seven of diamonds, East inserts the ten, and you win with the ace. You lead a trump to the ace and continue with the two of trumps from the table. East wins with the king and switches to the nine of spades, which you cover with the knave. West takes the queen and returns the knave of trumps to your queen. How do you continue?

There are eight top tricks, and the diamond suit will provide two more on a 3–2 break. But if West has no more diamonds East will be able to prevent the establishment of the suit by ducking when you run the nine. In that case the tenth trick will have to come from an end-play in spades, which will be possible only if you can first remove West's exit cards in clubs.

A singleton diamond would give West a 5–3–1–4 shape, and at first it looks impossible to remove four clubs from his hand. The play of the diamonds will apply pressure, however, provided that you make the key play of cashing the ace of clubs before leading the nine of diamonds. If West discards (presumably a spade), you must overtake with the knave of diamonds. East will have to hold off, and after ruffing a club you can lead a third diamond to the king. This time West will have to throw a club, since he cannot afford to part with another spade. A further club ruff will then extract his last

card in the suit, and the lead of the eight of spades will
produce a happy ending.

♠ A K Q 10 9 6
♡ K 10
◇ A Q 10   *Love all*
♣ J 5   *Dealer North*
                          N   S
♠ 7 2   1 ♠   1 NT
♡ 9 7 3 2   3 NT   —
◇ K J 5 4 3
♣ K 4

West leads the four of hearts against your contract of
three no trumps. You have nine sure tricks if West has led
away from the ace, and you do not wish to give East an
unnecessary chance to gain the lead, so you naturally go up
with the king. To your annoyance East produces the ace, and
to your relief he returns the eight of hearts to his partner's
knave. West switches to the nine of diamonds and you win in
dummy with the ace while East follows suit with the seven.
On your next play of the queen of diamonds East discards
the two of clubs. How should you continue?

There will be no problem if the spades break evenly, but
since West has length in both red suits he is quite likely to
have no more than one spade. That leaves you with a ninth
trick still to find.

The nine and seven of hearts are now equals, of course, and
it should be possible to create an extra trick by throwing
West in with a heart after running the diamonds. But the
throw-in will be effective only if you first remove West's
potential exit card in spades. To protect against the 4–1
spade break, therefore, you should cash one top spade at this
point. Then run the rest of the diamonds, discarding a club
and a spade from the table, and put West on lead with a
heart.

If West has no more spades he will have to yield the ninth

trick in either hearts or clubs, while if he has another spade to lead the suit will produce more than enough tricks for your contract.

The full hand:

```
                    ♠ A K Q 10 9 6
                    ♡ K 10
                    ◇ A Q 10
                    ♣ J 5
    ♠ 4                              ♠ J 8 5 3
    ♡ Q J 6 4        N               ♡ A 8 5
    ◇ 9 8 6 2     W     E            ◇ 7
    ♣ A 10 8 3       S              ♣ Q 9 7 6 2
                    ♠ 7 2
                    ♡ 9 7 3 2
                    ◇ K J 5 4 3
                    ♣ K 4
```

10. Playing the Odds

When faced with a choice between different ways of trying
for your contract, you will naturally attempt to select the
line of play that offers the best chance of success. Involved
calculations are neither possible nor desirable at the bridge
table, but a knowledge of simple probabilities can be useful.
If you know how your suits are likely to break, you will be
able to make an intelligent comparison of the chances of
various lines of play. This will help you to avoid the indignity
of going down by playing against the odds.

On certain hands the difference in merit between two lines
of play will be very wide, while on others it may be no more
than 3 per cent. Do not despise such small advantages. The
proprietors of gambling casinos grow fat and prosperous on
even smaller margins. If you are consistent in spotting plays
to give you a 3 per cent edge, you will be a big winner in the
long run.

Your first task when dummy goes down is to carry out a
careful review, first isolating and then comparing the various
lines of play that offer any prospect of making the contract.
Try to arrive at a rough probability figure for each, and
select your line of play on this basis when there is nothing
else to guide you. The simplest hands are those on which you
have no choice. If there is only one line of play that offers any
hope, you must adopt it no matter how slender the chance of
success. Any chance is better than none, but the trap of
embarking on a line of play that has no chance can only be
avoided by accurate analysis before playing a card.

The selection of the best line of play is often just a matter of common sense. Here is an example.

♠ A J 10 9
♡ 9 7 6 4
◇ 8 6   *Game all*
♣ J 5 2   *Dealer South*
                         S   N
♠ Q 5 4   2 NT   3 ♣
♡ A K   3 NT   —
◇ K Q 4
♣ A Q 10 9 4

West leads the five of diamonds, East plays the knave and you win with the king. How should you continue?

This is not a hand where you have to play for one of two finesses to be right. If you run the queen of spades at trick two you will certainly make your contract when the king is with West. When East has the spade king, however, you will go down if West started with five diamonds headed by the ace, as seems likely. The spade finesse therefore offers little more than a fifty-fifty chance.

Careful analysis indicates that if the spade finesse is right there is no need to take it. The club finesse is the vital one on this hand. The correct play at trick two is to lead the queen of spades and put on dummy's ace. The knave of clubs is returned for a finesse, and you are home if the suit produces five tricks. If West has the king of clubs you will succeed if he also has the king of spades, since your ninth trick will come from either diamonds or spades.

This line of play succeeds whenever the spade finesse is right. It also succeeds when the spade finesse is wrong if the clubs are good for five tricks, giving a total chance of over 68 per cent.

Note the importance of unblocking the spades by leading the queen at trick two. If West has a small singleton club you need a further entry to dummy to repeat the club finesse, and you may fail if you block the spades.

♠ 10 7
♡ A 9 7 4 3
◇ A K 4   *Game all*
♣ Q 9 6   *Dealer South*
           S   *N*
♠ A Q J 9 8 5 4   3 ♠   4 ♠
♡ 2
◇ 9 8 2
♣ 7 4

West leads the ace of clubs followed by the ten. You play low from dummy, but East overtakes with the knave and continues with the king of clubs. When you ruff with the eight of spades West follows suit with the three of clubs. What now?

A successful trump finesse will see you home if the trumps break no worse than 3–1. This gives a straight 45 per cent chance of success, but it may be possible to find better odds elsewhere. You can afford a loser in trumps if you can discard the losing diamond on a long heart, which should be possible on a 4–3 heart break. By deliberately giving up a trump trick you can create the extra entry needed in dummy.

The best play is a heart to the ace, followed by a heart ruffed high and a low trump from hand, conceding a trick to the king. You can win the diamond return in dummy, ruff another heart high, and return to the table by leading a trump to the ten. If the hearts behave kindly, a further ruff will establish the suit. You can then discard the losing diamond in dummy on your last trump and claim the last two tricks.

The probability of a 4–3 heart break is 62 per cent, but your play also hinges upon trumps breaking no worse than 3–1 and this reduces the overall chance of success to 56 per cent.

The defenders might have done better to switch to diamonds at trick three. This removes an entry prematurely and leaves you with no alternative to the trump finesse.

```
♠ K 8 7 4
♡ Q 10 8 3
◇ A 9                    Game all
♣ A K 6                  Dealer West
                 W      N      E       S
♠ —              1 ♠    Dbl    —       4 ♡
♡ A K J 9 5      —      6 ♡    All pass
◇ 10 8 6 2
♣ J 9 5 3
```

West leads the eight of clubs against your ambitious slam. How do you plan the play?

It is clear that partner does not have his bid, although he might retort that you hardly have yours. This is the sort of thing that is liable to happen when you are pressing for points.

The instinctive play is to guard against a club ruff by playing the ace on the first trick and drawing a round or two of trumps. A count of tricks shows this to be futile, however. The only possible winners in the side suits are three clubs and the ace of diamonds. The other eight tricks will have to come from trumps, which means that not more than one round can be played. Furthermore, you must lose the club trick to East before drawing a round of trumps. If you do it afterwards, he will be able to scupper the slam by leading a second trump.

All this leads to the conclusion that the slam can be made only if West has two clubs and precisely one trump. You should therefore play low from dummy at trick one and allow East to score his queen. Win the club return with the ace, cash the queen of hearts, then lead the king of clubs and hold your breath. When West discards, you can continue by cashing the ace of diamonds and ruffing a spade. After discarding the losing diamond from dummy on the knave of clubs, you will be able to cross-ruff the remainder for twelve tricks. There is no other way.

♠ A 3
♡ A J 10 9 4
◇ 10 8 2   *Love all*
♣ K 5 2   *Dealer South*
                  S   N
♠ K Q 7   2 NT   3 ♡
♡ K 7   3 NT   6 NT
◇ A K J 9 3
♣ A J 9

West leads the knave of spades against your slam. How do you plan the play?

It should be possible to combine your chances well if you start by finessing in one of the red suits. If the finesse wins, you can score twelve easy tricks by switching to the other suit. If the finesse loses, you will run the suit on regaining the lead and then cash the ace and king in the other red suit. As a last resort you will have the club finesse to fall back on for the twelfth trick.

The question of which suit to tackle first is answered by considering which queen is the more likely to drop. The frequency of a doubleton queen is clearly greater when there are five cards outstanding than when there are six. It is therefore in diamonds that you should try to drop the queen and in hearts that you should finesse.

The first trick should be won in hand, the king of hearts cashed, and a heart led to the nine. If East produces the queen, win the spade return with the ace and run the hearts, discarding three diamonds from your hand. Then cash the top diamonds to see if the queen drops, and cash your last spade, discarding a club from the table. If either opponent shows signs of discomfort you may decide to play for the queen of clubs to drop. Otherwise you will take the finesse at trick twelve. The play has an 84 per cent chance of success.

Reversing the order by finessing in diamonds and then trying to drop the queen of hearts would reduce your chance by about 3 per cent.

On many hands it is possible to combine the chances in several suits in this way.

♠ 6 4
♡ 10 9 5   *Game all*
◇ A K Q 8 3   *Dealer South*
♣ 9 7 2   S   N
                        1 ♣   1 ◇
♠ A K   2 ♡   3 ◇
♡ A J 3 2   3 NT   —
◇ 7 5
♣ A K 6 5 4

West leads the five of spades to the knave and king. There will be no trouble if the clubs behave reasonably, so you test the position by cashing the ace and king of clubs. Disappointingly, East discards the three of spades on the second round. What now?

There are two lines of play that seem to have a good deal of merit. The first is to duck a diamond immediately. That will succeed if the suit breaks no worse than 4–2, giving you 84 per cent for your money. The other method is to lead a diamond to the queen and return the ten of hearts for a finesse. If West wins and knocks out the ace of spades, you can test the diamonds for a 3–3 break and if that fails take a further heart finesse. The chance of success for this play, oddly enough, is also in the neighbourhood of 84 per cent.

So far we have been considering each suit in isolation, but when we apply probabilities within the context of the whole hand the choice of plays is made easy for us. The fact that East showed out on the second round of clubs marks him with most of the red cards, and this is enough to swing the balance firmly in favour of the second line of play.

♠ K Q 9 8 6
♡ A 7 4   *Game all*
◇ 8 7 3   *Dealer South*
♣ 6 3   S   N
                      1 ◇   1 ♠
♠ J 7   2 NT   3 ◇
♡ K 9 6   3 NT   —
◇ A J 10 5
♣ A K Q 2

West leads the knave of clubs to your queen. How do you plan the play?

The problem here is to combine the chances in spades and diamonds in the optimum way. The obvious method of play is to lead the knave of spades at trick two. If this is won by the ace you will have an easy path to nine tricks. So the defenders will presumably allow the knave of spades to win, and you will continue with a spade to the queen. If this also wins, you can switch to diamonds with good chances. If East wins the second spade, however, you will win the heart switch in dummy, test the spades for a 3–3 break, and if that fails lead a diamond, succeeding if East has both diamond honours or one honour with shortage. The combination of chances produced by this line of play add up to a healthy 80 per cent.

Better odds can be obtained, however, by leading the seven of spades to dummy's eight at trick two. If East wins the trick it will be a simple matter to establish the three spade tricks you need for the contract. To create a problem, therefore, the opponents must hold off, but you can now use the extra entry to dummy to take a diamond finesse. You will win the heart switch in hand with the king, lead the knave of spades to the queen and ace, win the next heart in dummy and test the spades. When the suit fails to break you will be in the position to take a second diamond finesse, making your contract unless West has both diamond honours. The chance of success for this line of play is no less than 90 per cent.

♠ 6 2	*Game all*	
♡ 4	*Dealer North*	
◇ A Q 10 6 3	*N*	*S*
♣ A K 8 4 3	1 ◇	2 ♡
	3 ♣	3 ♡
♠ A 7 3	4 ♣	4 NT
♡ A K Q J 9 2	5 ♡	5 NT
◇ K 8	6 ◇	7 ♡
♣ 7 2		

West leads the king of spades, East plays the knave and you win with the ace. You cash the ace and king of trumps, discarding a spade from the table. Both opponents follow suit, but when you continue with a third round of trumps West throws a spade. How do you plan the play?

You can combine your chances in clubs and diamonds by discarding one card from each suit on the third and fourth trumps. A third-round club ruff will then enable you to take advantage of a 3–3 break in the suit, while you still retain the chance of finding the diamonds 3–3 or dropping the knave. Provided that you play off the last trump before testing the diamonds, there is also the possibility of a minor-suit squeeze against West, bringing the total chance of success for this line of play to about 75 per cent.

The best percentage does not always come from combination play, however. In this case the odds favour ignoring the clubs and concentrating on the diamond suit. You should discard two clubs on the trumps and then play diamonds, cashing the king, ace and queen and ruffing the fourth round if necessary. This line succeeds when the diamonds break no worse than 4–2 and when the knave is a singleton. The minor-suit squeeze is still a possibility, and the chance of success is about 87 per cent.

```
♠ K Q 4
♡ A 8 6 3
◇ Q 5                    E–W game
♣ A 9 5 3               Dealer North
                         N        S
♠ A J 7                 1 NT      3 ♡
♡ K 10 9 5 4            4 ♣       6 ♡
◇ A 7
♣ K Q 8
```

West leads the knave of diamonds against your small slam.
East covers the queen with his king and you win the trick
with the ace. Hoping to avoid a trump loser, you lead a low
heart from hand. West promptly dashes your hopes by discarding the six of diamonds. After winning with the ace, how
do you proceed?

A trump loser is inevitable and it is clear that you must
find a way of disposing of your small diamond before allowing East to gain the lead. A 3–3 club break will not help you
here. East would simply ruff the fourth club with his small
heart, and you would be left with a loser in both trumps and
diamonds.

You are forced to the conclusion that the slam can be
made only if East has to follow to four rounds of clubs. Yet
you need to score four tricks in the suit. One chance is to
play West for the knave and ten doubleton, but a small
doubleton is six times as likely. When East plays a low card
on your lead of the three of clubs, therefore, you should cross
your fingers and finesse the eight. If this holds and East has
to follow to four rounds of clubs you will get your losing
diamond away and concede only a trump trick.

The play risks going two down, of course, but that is a
small price to pay for a chance of making the slam.

♠ 7 6 2
♡ K 6
◇ 8 4   *Love all*
♣ A K 9 8 4 3   *Dealer South*

	S	N
♠ A J 5 4	1 ◇	2 ♣
♡ A 9 5	3 NT	—
◇ A Q J 6 3		
♣ Q		

West leads the four of hearts against your contract of three no trumps. How do you plan the play?

The first move, naturally, is to win the trick with the ace in order to preserve the king as a later entry to dummy. Now there are several ways of combining the chances in the minor suits. One possibility is to unblock the queen of clubs at trick two and continue with the queen of diamonds from hand. This line of play will succeed when either minor suit breaks 3–3 and also when the knave and ten of clubs are doubleton, giving a chance of success of 61 per cent.

Alternatively, you may decide to overtake the queen of clubs with the king and cash the ace. If both defenders follow suit and the ten or knave appears, you can make sure of nine tricks by continuing with the nine of clubs. If no club honour appears, or if either defender shows out on the first or second round, you can switch to diamonds, making the contract when that suit breaks 3–3 or when East has a doubleton king. This is an improvement, yielding a total chance of 68 per cent.

The third possibility is to overtake the club queen and to continue the suit if the defenders follow to two rounds whether an honour card appears or not. Strangely enough, if both defenders play small clubs on the first two rounds the chances are better than even that the suit will break 3–3. The club continuation is therefore superior to the diamond switch, giving a total chance of 72 per cent.

♠ A 8 4
♡ 4 3
◊ A 8 7 3   *N–S game*
♣ 9 4 3 2   *Dealer South*

	S	N
♠ K Q 6 3	1 ♡	1 NT
♡ A K 9 8 5 2	3 ♡	4 ♡
◊ K 6		
♣ 6		

West leads the queen of clubs and continues with the knave, East echoing with the eight and the five. After ruffing, how do you continue?

The problem is to avoid a spade loser in the event of a 4–1 trump break. Squeeze chances are negligible because you cannot concede trump tricks without being forced in clubs. You could cater for a singleton trump and short spades in the same hand by cashing one round of trumps and then three rounds of spades. This would enable you to ruff the fourth spade in dummy, losing only two hearts and a club.

This plan will not work, however, in the more likely event of the player with four trumps being short in spades. He would ruff the second or third spade and lead a trump, and you would be left with four losers.

The best percentage is obtained by playing three rounds of spades before touching trumps. If an opponent ruffs the third spade and returns a trump, you will still be able to ruff the small spade in dummy and make ten tricks.

To avoid risk when the trumps are 3–2, however, you must give careful thought to the order in which you play the spades. If you allow East to ruff a spade honour and a club comes back, there will be a danger of an over-ruff by West on the next round. You can cash a top trump and lead another spade, but if East started with three trumps he will ruff and lead another club to promote his partner's last trump.

You can overcome this hazard by leading a spade to the

ace and a spade back to your king. If East ruffs on the second round he will be ruffing a loser and you will simply draw trumps. If both defenders follow to the second spade, you should re-enter dummy with the ace of diamonds and lead a third spade. Again East cannot profitably ruff, and you will lose three tricks at most. You do not mind if West ruffs a spade honour, of course, for he can make no damaging return.

Two possible hands for the opponents are shown below.

```
              ♠ A 8 4
              ♡ 4 3
              ◇ A 8 7 3
              ♣ 9 4 3 2
♠ 10 2                        ♠ J 9 7 5
♡ Q 10 7 6          N         ♡ J
◇ J 9 5         W       E     ◇ Q 10 4 2
♣ Q J 10 7          S         ♣ A K 8 5
              ♠ K Q 6 3
              ♡ A K 9 8 5 2
              ◇ K 6
              ♣ 6
```

The percentage play pays off when you find a defender with four hearts and two spades.

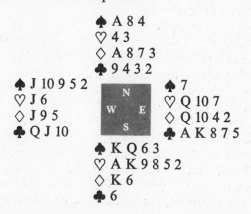

```
              ♠ A 8 4
              ♡ 4 3
              ◇ A 8 7 3
              ♣ 9 4 3 2
♠ J 10 9 5 2                  ♠ 7
♡ J 6              N          ♡ Q 10 7
◇ J 9 5        W      E       ◇ Q 10 4 2
♣ Q J 10          S          ♣ A K 8 7 5
              ♠ K Q 6 3
              ♡ A K 9 8 5 2
              ◇ K 6
              ♣ 6
```

And the contract is still safe when the trumps are 3–2 provided that you take care not to let East ruff a spade honour.

♠ Q 10 8 4
♡ K 10 3
◇ K 7 3   *Game all*
♣ K 6 4   *Dealer South*
                        S   N
♠ K J 9 7 2   1 ♠   3 ♠
♡ Q 6 2   4 ♠   —
◇ A J 6
♣ A 5

West leads the knave of clubs and you win in hand with the ace. You lead a small spade to the queen and ace, win the return of the queen of clubs with the king, and ruff the third club with the knave of spades, both opponents following suit. The outstanding trumps fall when you lead the nine of spades to dummy's ten. How should you continue?

There must be excellent chances of avoiding three losers in the red suits. It seems reasonable to start by leading a small heart to the queen. Whether this wins or loses, you may as well play the king of hearts on the second round. If West has the knave he will be end-played on the third round, forced to yield the tenth trick no matter what he returns. If the knave of hearts is with East you can always fall back on the diamond finesse. This line gives a 74 per cent chance of success.

Better odds can be obtained by tackling the diamonds first, however. The correct play is to cash the ace and king of diamonds and continue with the knave. If East has the queen, or West the queen doubleton, the hand is over. And if West is able to win the third diamond he will have to return a heart, giving you a free finesse of the ten. You will therefore make the game when West has either the ace or the knave of hearts. The overall chance of success for this line of play is 89 per cent.

The best play was not found when the hand turned up in the English European Championship Trials of 1974.

♠ 10 3
♡ A K 10
♢ A 5 2
♣ J 7 6 4 2

♠ A Q J 9 4
♡ 8 4 3
♢ Q 3
♣ K 5 3

	S	W	N	E
	1 ♠	Dbl	Rdbl	—
	—	2 ♢	—	—
	2 ♠	—	3 ♢	—
	3 NT	*All pass*		

N–S game
Dealer South

West leads the knave of diamonds and you play low from dummy. East wins with the king and returns the eight of diamonds to your queen. How do you plan the play?

You are no doubt wishing that your partner had been less forward in the bidding, since the prospects in three no trumps are far from hopeful. Five spade tricks can be made only if West has three small cards in the suit, and you have to reject this possibility in the light of the bidding. Even four spade tricks will be difficult to make because of the paucity of entries in your hand. You are forced to the conclusion that it can be done only if West has the king singleton or doubleton.

Four spades will bring your tally up to eight tricks. The ninth trick will have to come from hearts, since there is no time to develop the clubs. At trick three, therefore, you should lead a heart and put in the ten when West plays low. If that passes off successfully you can run the ten of spades. Even if West plays low on this trick you should stick to your plan, putting up the ace on the second round and hoping for the king to fall on your left.

It may not be much of a chance, but it is your only one.

♠ J 8 4
♡ K J 6 4
◇ Q J 5 2   *Love all*
♣ A Q   *Dealer South*
                   S   N
♠ Q 10 3   1 NT   2 ♣
♡ A 9 5 2   2 ♡   4 ♡
◇ A K 7
♣ 9 4 3

West begins with the ace, king and another spade, and it
is a relief when East follows suit three times. What do you
play at trick four?

If there is a trump loser you cannot afford a club loser, and
vice versa. It may therefore occur to you to clarify the position by taking the club finesse at once. When the queen of
clubs wins you can afford a safety play in trumps, playing the
king on the first round and then leading the four to your
nine. This protects against all 4–1 trump breaks. When the
club finesse loses, you will need to play for no trump loser.
The optimum method is a low trump from hand, finessing
the knave when West plays low. This succeeds when the
trumps are 3–2 and the queen with West, and also when West
has the singleton queen. On the face of it the chance of
success for this line of play is about 66 per cent, but it reduces
to 63 per cent because of the possibility of an uppercut in
spades when the club finesse loses.

You can, in fact, get better odds by playing trumps first.
The correct play is a heart to the king and a heart back to the
ace. If both defenders follow suit and the queen does not
drop, continue with four rounds of diamonds and then, in
the absence of a ruff, lead a trump.

This line of play succeeds whenever East has three trumps,
when East has a doubleton queen, and when West has a
singleton queen. And if the club finesse is right it also succeeds when East has a small doubleton trump and when West

has any four trumps or a singleton ten, giving a total chance
of success of 69 per cent.

♠ K 4
♡ Q 10 8 3
◊ A Q 8 2   *N–S game*
♣ 10 9 3   *Dealer South*

		S	W	N	E
♠ A		1 ♡	1 ♠	3 ♡	4 ♠
♡ A K J 6 4 2		5 ♡	*All pass*		
◊ 6 4 3					
♣ A J 5					

West leads the queen of spades to your ace. Both opponents follow suit when you cash the ace of hearts. How
should you proceed?

It seems a reasonable move to win the second trump in
dummy, cash the king of spades for a diamond discard, and
run the ten of clubs. When West wins he will have to return
a diamond to avoid giving you the eleventh trick immediately. If the diamond finesse loses East will no doubt return
a club, thereby denying you the option of testing for 3–3
diamonds. Still, you will fail only when West has both club
honours and East the diamond king, which gives you a
respectable 88 per cent chance of success.

Can you see anything better? It is an improvement, in
fact, to win the second trump in hand and take an immediate
diamond finesse. If East has the king he will switch to clubs,
and after winning a club trick West will be able to exit in
either spades or diamonds. The difference is that you now
have the chance to test the diamonds for a 3–3 split before
committing yourself to a second club finesse, and this boosts
your chances to 92 per cent.

But it would hardly be logical to chase after a 92 per cent
chance when 100 per cent odds are available. The sure way of
making the contract is to win the second trump in either
hand, cash the ace of diamonds, take a diamond discard on

the king of spades, and continue with a low diamond from the table. If West wins the trick he will be end-played immediately. If East wins and leads another diamond you can discard a club from hand and the queen of diamonds will provide the eleventh trick. If East wins and returns a club you can play low, and West will have to yield the eleventh trick whether he returns a club, a diamond or a spade.

The full hand:

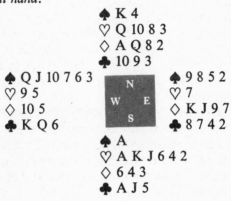

```
                    ♠ K 4
                    ♡ Q 10 8 3
                    ◇ A Q 8 2
                    ♣ 10 9 3
  ♠ Q J 10 7 6 3          ♠ 9 8 5 2
  ♡ 9 5              N     ♡ 7
  ◇ 10 5          W   E   ◇ K J 9 7
  ♣ K Q 6            S     ♣ 8 7 4 2
                    ♠ A
                    ♡ A K J 6 4 2
                    ◇ 6 4 3
                    ♣ A J 5
```

11. All in Good Time

In the play of the hand the dividing line between success and failure can be a narrow one. You may hold all the right cards and yet fail to make your contract if you play them in the wrong order. Accurate timing is needed in so many different situations that it is hard to present the subject in isolation. The example hands are likely to range over the entire field of card-play technique.

The time factor can be vital in deals that call for normal suit establishment, in those that require careful trump management, and in those involving communication plays of all kinds. It is prominent especially in cross-ruff situations, in deals where the trumps are working hard, and of course in the preparation of advanced endings such as throw-ins, trump coups and squeezes.

Faulty timing can invariably be traced to a lack of early planning. Declarers tend to take the easy, optimistic view at trick one, predicating their play on the assumption of normal suit breaks and docile opponents. Naturally, a sequence of play designed to cope with favourable breaks and pedestrian defence is likely to prove inadequate in the face of an adverse break or an astute switch. It is only when the unexpected happens that the declarer wakes up to the fact that his timing is hopelessly wrong.

The recipe for success does not change. To achieve precise timing you must carry out your chores before playing to the first trick. Send out mental radar signals to probe the shape of the obstacles that lie ahead. You may then be able to take evasive action in good time.

It takes an improbable defence and distribution to defeat the contract on this first example. But it is easy enough to defeat yourself.

♠ A 6 4
♡ 3   *Love all*
♢ 6 4 3   *Dealer South*
♣ K Q J 10 9 5

	S	N
	1 ♡	2 ♣
♠ K Q 2	2 ♢	3 ♣
♡ K Q J 5 2	3 NT	—
♢ K J 10 8		
♣ 4		

West leads the knave of spades against your contract of three no trumps. How do you plan the play?

You will naturally win the first trick in hand in order to preserve a later entry for the clubs. But if you give the hand no more than a cursory analysis you may fall into the trap of leading the club at trick two. Do you see what will happen if you do? A spade will come back and you will have to win in dummy in order to retain a spade entry to your hand. You will therefore have no option but to cash your club tricks straight away, which will embarrass you seriously. You may choose to part with three hearts and two diamonds, but this leaves you in danger of defeat if West has both diamond honours or if you make the wrong guess when a diamond is led by East. Nor will it help to leave one or two club winners in dummy. When the cards are badly placed the defenders will always be able to hold you to eight tricks.

A count of winners tells you that you need a trick from hearts as well as five clubs, and correct timing requires that the king of hearts be led at trick two. You can win the spade return in hand, cash one high heart for a discard of a diamond from the table, and lead a club. The contract will then be at risk only if East is able to hold up the ace of clubs until the fifth round.

♠ 8 3
♡ K 6 4
◇ J 7 4
♣ A K 8 6 3

W	N	E	S
1 ◇	—	—	Dbl

♠ A Q 7
♡ A Q 8 7 2
◇ 10 5
♣ Q 4 2

Game all
Dealer West

W	N	E	S
—	3 ♣	—	3 ♡
—	4 ♡	All pass	

West attacks with the three top diamonds, East following suit as you ruff the third round. How should you continue?

There will be eleven easy tricks if both hearts and clubs break 3–2, but that is less than an even chance. The likelihood is that one of the suits will split 4–1 and you should plan the play on this assumption. If it is the clubs that break 4–1 you can safeguard the contract by ducking a round of clubs after drawing trumps. Similarly, if the hearts are 4–1 you can succeed by ducking the first or second round of hearts. But you would look silly if you ducked a heart and subsequently found the hearts 3–2 and the clubs 4–1.

There is no way of making the contract if both suits break badly, but correct timing will succeed when either suit is 4–1. The proper sequence of play is to cash the ace and queen of hearts at tricks four and five. If both defenders follow suit you can draw the last trump and duck a club. If either defender shows out on the second round of trumps you must switch to clubs, relying on a 3–2 break in that suit. The defender with the long trumps may ruff on the third or fourth round of clubs, but that will be the last trick for the defence. You will be able to win any return in hand and lead a trump. The king of hearts in dummy serves a double purpose, drawing the last trump and providing entry to the remaining clubs.

♠ Q 6
♡ 5 3 2   *Game all*
◇ 10 5 3 2   *Dealer South*
♣ A 6 4 3   S   N
                          1 ♠   1 NT
♠ A K 5 4 3   3 ♡   3 ♠
♡ A K J 8   4 ♠   —
◇ Q
♣ K 10 2

West leads the queen of clubs, East plays the five and you win with the king. How do you plan the play?

On a 3–3 trump break you will have nine top tricks, and the tenth trick may come from the long club, the long heart or the heart finesse. Trumps are more likely to break 4–2, however, in which case you will need the heart finesse *and* a 3–3 break in one of the side suits if you are to make the contract. And if you are going to avail yourself of the chance of a 3–3 club break you will have to concede the second round of the suit. This in turn will involve leaving the enemy master trump at large, since you cannot afford to be forced twice in diamonds.

Projecting the play a stage further you can see that when you eventually arrive in dummy with the ace of clubs you may wish to cash the thirteenth club, not caring whether a defender ruffs with the master trump or not. It is clear, therefore, that the heart finesse must not be postponed until that late stage. To get the timing right you must take the heart finesse when you are first in dummy with the queen of spades. The correct sequence is king of clubs, spade to queen, heart finesse, spade ace and spade king. If a defender shows out on the third spade you still lead and pass the ten of clubs. After ruffing the second diamond you can continue with a club to the ace, and if the suit breaks 3–3 you scramble home by discarding your small heart on the thirteenth club.

It is not easy to foresee the need for an early heart finesse,

and when the hand turned up in a European Championship
match between Britain and Switzerland in 1967 both declarers went astray. The full hand was as follows.

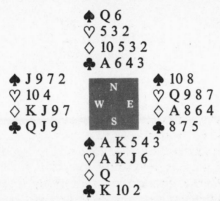

```
                    ♠ Q 6
                    ♡ 5 3 2
                    ◇ 10 5 3 2
                    ♣ A 6 4 3
   ♠ J 9 7 2                      ♠ 10 8
   ♡ 10 4          N              ♡ Q 9 8 7
   ◇ K J 9 7    W     E           ◇ A 8 6 4
   ♣ Q J 9         S              ♣ 8 7 5
                    ♠ A K 5 4 3
                    ♡ A K J 6
                    ◇ Q
                    ♣ K 10 2
```

The play developed on similar lines in both rooms. The
club lead was won with the king, three rounds of spades
were cashed, and a club was ducked. The West players
avoided the mistake of cashing the master trump and
switched to diamonds. The second diamond was ruffed and
a club led to the ace in the position shown below.

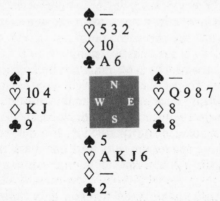

```
                    ♠ —
                    ♡ 5 3 2
                    ◇ 10
                    ♣ A 6
   ♠ J                            ♠ —
   ♡ 10 4          N              ♡ Q 9 8 7
   ◇ K J        W     E           ◇ 8
   ♣ 9              S              ♣ 8
                    ♠ 5
                    ♡ A K J 6
                    ◇ —
                    ♣ 2
```

The declarers were then unable to take advantage of the

favourable club break without giving up the chance of the
heart finesse. It is a trappy hand.

♠ 6 5
♡ 10 6   *Match-point pairs*
◇ A 6 4 3 2   *Game all*
♣ A Q 7 5   *Dealer South*
                          S   N
♠ A J 9   1 ♡   2 ◇
♡ A Q 5 3   3 NT   —
◇ K 8
♣ K 6 4 2

The lead of the king of spades draws the five from dummy,
the four from East and the nine from you. West switches to
the queen of diamonds, and again you play low from both
hands as East follows with the five. The knave of diamonds
comes next, East plays the nine and you win with the king.
How should you continue?

Since you can develop at least one extra trick in diamonds
you can be sure of nine tricks when the clubs are 3–2. And if
West has four diamonds, as seems likely, you will be able to
make your contract even when the clubs are 4–1 by throwing
West in to make a major suit return. The same throw-in will
produce an overtrick when the clubs are 3–2, but a little care
will be needed in the timing of the play.

Suppose you lead a club to the queen and cash the ace of
diamonds to find East showing out. You will then want to
remove the clubs from the West hand before effecting the
throw-in, but you will be unable to do so in safety. A 4–1
club break will leave you with no entry to the long diamond.

The remedy is very simple. You must cash the king of clubs
before leading a low club to the queen. You will thus discover the club situation in good time, and if the break is
favourable you will be able to try for the overtrick without
placing the contract at risk.

♠ 8 7 5 4
♡ K 6 4
◇ A Q 8 2   *Game all*
♣ J 6   *Dealer South*
                        S   N
♠ A K 6 2   1 NT   2 ♣
♡ A 7 5 2   2 ♠   4 ♠
◇ 6 4
♣ A Q 10

West leads the three of spades, East plays the queen and you win with the ace. How should you continue?

You will need one of the minor suit finesses to be right if there are two trump losers, but to judge from the play to the first trick it is unlikely that the trumps are 4–1. If trumps are 3–2 is there any danger? Not unless your timing is careless. Even with both finesses wrong and the hearts failing to break, you should be able to make the contract provided that you do not permit an opponent to draw the third round of trumps.

The opening lead provides the clue to the correct line of play. Since West would hardly lead the small trump from a doubleton, he is marked with the trump length. In that case it could be fatal to lose an early trick to East. A losing diamond finesse would allow East to knock out your king of spades, and the loss of a subsequent club finesse would enable West to hold you to nine tricks by drawing the third round of trumps.

To get the timing right you should cross to dummy with the king of hearts at trick two and run the knave of clubs. If West produces the king and returns a trump, you can win and take the diamond finesse. East may win but, lacking a third trump, he will be unable to stop you scoring ten tricks on a cross-ruff.

♠ A Q 10 9 5
♡ 9 5
◇ 3
♣ 10 8 6 5 3

Love all
Dealer West

W	N	E	S
1 ♡	2 ♡*	—	4 ♠
All pass			

♠ 8 6 2
♡ K 7 3
◇ A J 6
♣ A K 7 4

* Weak black two-suiter

West leads the queen of clubs, East plays the two and you win with the ace. How do you plan the play?

If the queen of clubs is a singleton you will need to find West with both spade honours. To run the eight of spades would be to take too strong a position, however. The clubs may be 2–2 or West may have three. In the latter case you can afford a trump loser if you can avoid the loss of more than one heart, which may be possible when West has the king of spades and no more than three diamonds.

At trick two, therefore, you should finesse the queen of spades. Then cash the spade ace, lead a diamond to your ace, ruff a diamond in dummy and return a club. If East has the outstanding trump it will do him no good to ruff, so you will win with the king and ruff another diamond. Then exit with a club and hope for the best. If West is out of diamonds he will have to open up the hearts, providing you with a tenth trick. The East-West cards:

♠ K 4
♡ A Q 10 6 2
◇ K 7 4
♣ Q J 9

♠ J 7 3
♡ J 8 4
◇ Q 10 9 8 5 2
♣ 2

This hand was played as described by Jeremy Flint in the Eastbourne Spring Foursomes of 1972.

♠ A Q 9	*Game all*		
♡ 10	*Dealer East*		
◇ A K Q 3	W	N	E	S
♣ A K 8 7 3			1 ♡	—
	2 ♡	Dbl	3 ♡	—
♠ 8 6 4	—	Dbl	—	4 ◇
♡ Q 5 4	—	4 NT	—	5 ♣
◇ J 10 6 5 2	—	5 ◇	All pass	
♣ 6 2				

West leads the ace of hearts and switches to the five of
spades. You try the nine from dummy but East wins the trick
with the ten. You win his return of the nine of diamonds in
dummy with the ace, West following suit with the four. How
should you continue?

East is likely to have the king of spades, so you will have
to establish a long club to take care of your loser. You will
also need two heart ruffs in dummy to bring your total up
to eleven tricks. Naturally, you will have no trouble if the
trumps break 2–2 or the clubs 3–3.

Favourable breaks should not be expected, however. If the
trumps are 3–1 and the clubs 4–2 careful timing will be
needed to ensure that you do not establish the long club too
soon. The correct move at trick four is to lead the three of
diamonds to your ten. If trumps prove to be 3–1, you must
ruff a heart before starting on the clubs. When you ruff the
third club you will know the whole story. If the suit breaks
evenly you can draw the last trump and discard your spade
and heart losers on the established clubs. And if clubs are 4–2
you can ruff your third heart, ruff another club, and draw the
last trump with the knave, discarding the queen of spades
from the table.

You are in good company if you had a blind spot. In a
Camrose match between Scotland and England five diamonds
failed in both rooms when the play was mistimed.

♠ A 10 9 3
♡ 9 8 7 2   *Love all*
♢ A Q 6   *Dealer South*
♣ 8 2

	S	N
	1 ♢	1 ♡
♠ 6	2 ♣	3 ♢
♡ A K 4	4 ♡	5 ♢
♢ K J 8 4 3		
♣ A 9 7 5		

West leads the two of spades to dummy's ace, and your first thought is that you have missed an easy three no trumps. How do you proceed in five diamonds?

There are four tricks in the side suits, leaving seven to be scored from trumps. To avoid an over-ruff on the third round of clubs you may need to ruff high in dummy, which will necessitate scoring the five trumps in your hand separately. The easiest way to do this is by ruffing spades, and you will have to watch the timing.

The correct technique is to ruff a spade at trick two and then duck a club. Win any return in hand, cash the top hearts and the ace of clubs, and ruff a club high. A spade ruff is followed by a high ruff of the fourth club, and a further spade ruff with the eight of diamonds produces eleven tricks.

This hand was played by Claude Rodrigue in the 1971 European Championships. The East–West cards:

♠ Q 7 5 2   ♠ K J 8 4
♡ Q 10 6 3 ♡ J 5
♢ —   ♢ 10 9 7 5 2
♣ Q 10 6 4 3 ♣ K J

Three no trumps was not on, but five diamonds rolled home in spite of the 5–0 trump break.

♠ A J 10
♡ Q 10 6 5   *Game all*
◇ A 8 7 4   *Dealer South*
♣ 6 3   S   N
                         1 ♠   2 ◇
♠ K Q 7 6 3 2   3 ♣   4 ♠
♡ 8   4 NT   5 ♡
◇ K 5   6 ♠   —
♣ A K 7 5

West leads the queen of clubs, East plays the four and you win with the ace. How should you continue?

With trumps no worse than 3–1, you should be able to make the slam by ruffing the two losing clubs in dummy. You would have to take care to avoid an over-ruff on the third round of diamonds, but you could do that easily enough by exiting with a heart after ruffing the last club in dummy.

But suppose you run into a 4–0 trump break. In that case you cannot afford to ruff twice in dummy unless you can score three small trumps in your hand by ruffing. And that will be possible only if you get the timing right by leading your heart at trick two. You can win a trump return in dummy, and if the 4–0 break comes to light you can ruff a heart straight away. The king and ace of diamonds can be followed by another heart ruff, then the king of clubs and a club ruff.

At this point you will be home if it is East who has the trumps, for he will be the victim of a coup on the lead of any red card from dummy. If West has the trumps you must hope that he has a red card left and that you can guess the right suit to lead from the table. The fall of the cards so far should give some indication. At any rate you will have a play for your contract, whereas you would have had little chance if you had ruffed a club at trick three.

The study of these cross-ruff situations can be of great

value in sharpening your sense of timing. The next hand is
of similar type.

```
♠ K Q 2
♡ A 7 6 4        Game all
♢ A Q 4 2        Dealer North
♣ 6 5             N        S
                  1 ♡      2 ♢
♠ 7               3 ♢      4 NT
♡ K 3             5 ♡      6 ♢
♢ K J 10 5 3
♣ A K 10 4 2
```

West leads the knave of spades against your contract of
six diamonds. When you cover with the queen East takes his
ace and returns the queen of clubs. You win with the ace and
cash the king of diamonds, on which West discards a spade.
How should you continue?

Once again the bad trump break means that you must plan
to score the small trumps in your hand by ruffing, and this
will be possible only when East has at least three hearts. You
will need to ruff the third club high in case East has only two
cards in the suit, but you must not do it too early or East
may be able to make a deadly discard.

The correct sequence is the heart king, a heart to the ace,
the spade king for a club discard, and a heart ruff. Then cash
the king of clubs and ruff a club with the queen of diamonds.
If the clubs break evenly you can simply draw trumps at this
point. If East discards a spade on the third round of clubs,
however, you must make up your mind, having regard to the
earlier play in hearts, whether you can now ruff a spade or a
heart with your remaining small trump.

♠ A 7 6
♡ K 9   *Game all*
◇ K J 10 6 5 2   *Dealer South*
♣ K 5   S   W   N   E
                                            1 ♡   1 ♠   2 ◇   —
♠ 3   3 ♣   —   3 ♠   —
♡ A Q 8 6 3 2   4 ♣   —   4 NT   —
◇ Q   5 ♡   —   6 ♡   *All pass*
♣ A Q J 10 3

West leads the king of spades to dummy's ace. How do you
plan the play?

Only a bad trump break can endanger the slam. There is
nothing that can be done when West has four trumps, but
when East has four there is a chance if West's singleton is an
honour card. You will be able to engineer a trump coup
against East only if you take the proper precautions in good
time, however. Your trump holding must be reduced to the
same length as East's, which involves ruffing twice in your
hand.

The first step in this direction should be taken at trick two
by ruffing a spade. Then cash the ace of hearts and lead the
queen of diamonds to knock out the ace. If a club is returned
you must take care to win in hand, continuing with a trump
to the king and another spade ruff. On a normal trump break
you can draw the last trump and claim the remainder of the
tricks. But if West has shown up with a singleton trump
honour, you can enter dummy with the king of clubs and run
the diamonds to pick up East's trumps.

The execution of a trump coup is by no means difficult.
The problem is mainly one of recognition. It is easy to get
the timing wrong if the possibilities are not seen from the
outset.

♠ 9 8 4 2   *Game all*
♡ K 8 4   *Dealer South*
◇ Q 6   *S*   *N*
♣ 9 7 3 2   2 ♣   2 ◇
                      2 ♡   3 ♡
♠ A   3 ♠   4 ♡
♡ A J 7 6 5 2   5 ♣   5 ◇
◇ A K 5   6 ♡   —
♣ A K 6

West leads the knave of diamonds against your contract of six hearts. How do you plan the play?

This is no better than a fair slam. You will naturally take your best chance by playing for the drop in trumps if the queen does not appear on the first round. When either defender has a small singleton trump you will go down, therefore. And what if someone is void in trumps? You might expect to go two down, but this is not inevitable. Strangely enough, 4–0 may be better than 3–1 on this hand. If the defender with four trumps has a particular distribution—four spades, three diamonds and two clubs—it will be possible to make the slam by using the familiar trump coup technique.

The ending must be envisaged before a card is played from dummy if the timing is to be right. In order to conserve entries you must play the six of diamonds from the table and win the first trick in hand. Then unblock the ace of spades before leading a trump to the king. If either defender shows out you can ruff a spade, lead the five of diamonds to the queen, and ruff another spade. Cash the ace and king of clubs, re-enter dummy by ruffing your high diamond, and ruff another spade. If all has gone well you will be left with the ace and knave of hearts and the six of clubs, while an opponent has the three outstanding trumps. You simply exit with the club and table your cards.

If East has the trumps you will also succeed when his shape is 3–4–4–2.

♠ A K Q J 10 3
♡ 6   *Game all*
◇ K J 10 6   *Dealer North*
♣ A Q   N   S
                               2 ♣   2 ♡
♠ 5   2 ♠   3 ◇
♡ A J 10 5 4   4 ◇   4 NT
◇ A 9 7 3   5 ♣   6 ◇
♣ J 4 2

The five-club response to your Byzantine four no trump
inquiry shows two aces and the king of trumps. It denies the
queen of trumps, so you are not tempted to try for seven.
West leads the six of clubs and you put up the ace. Both
defenders follow with low cards when you lead a diamond to
your ace. How should you continue?

Naturally you will not plan to finesse in trumps on the way
back. The percentage play is to go up with the king and
switch to spades, hoping to get your clubs away before a
defender can ruff. In this way you will make your contract
when the queen of trumps drops and when either defender
has three trumps to the queen and at least two spades.

Are there any extra chances? You are sure to go down
when West has four trumps. If you play a third round of
trumps he will play a fourth, leaving you a trick short. And
if you ignore the two outstanding trumps he will score them
both. But what if East has four trumps? You will have some
chance of a coup by running the spades through him, discarding two clubs and three hearts from your hand. A heart
to the ace and a heart ruff will then bring your total up to
twelve tricks.

Do you see the snag? East may foil this plan by discarding
all his hearts on the spades. Then he will be able to ruff your
heart lead with his small diamond and cash the queen of
diamonds to beat the slam. To rectify the timing of the
possible trump coup, therefore, you must make the far-

sighted play of cashing the ace of hearts before leading a second trump.

		♠ Q 9			
		♡ A 3	*Love all*		
		◇ A J 10 6 3	*Dealer West*		
		♣ Q J 10 5	*W*	*N*	*E*	*S*

♠ Q 9
♡ A 3   *Love all*
◇ A J 10 6 3   *Dealer West*
♣ Q J 10 5   *W*   *N*   *E*   *S*
                  3 ♠   —   —   4 ♣*
♠ A K   —   4 ♠   —   5 ♣
♡ K J 7 5 2   —   6 ♣   *All pass*
◇ 4
♣ A 9 7 3 2

                  * *For take-out*

West leads the knave of spades to your ace, East following suit with the six. After a diamond to the ace you run the queen of clubs hopefully, but West produces the king and returns a club to the knave. East discards the two of spades on the second club, and he discards the four of hearts when you continue with the ten of clubs. What now?

West is marked with ten cards in the black suits, and it is clear that you have some sort of cross-ruff squeeze position against East. The heart finesse is certainly likely to be right, but you must avoid the mistake of testing the hearts prematurely.

Correct timing calls for the ruff of a diamond at this point. The diamond ruff will serve the dual purpose of helping to count the hand and setting up the squeeze position. The lead of the king of spades will then elicit a red card and a low moan from East. Your count of the distribution will be complete when you lead a heart to the ace and you will know which red suit can be ruffed out.

In cross-ruff squeeze situations it is usually right to aim for a position where you have the same number of trumps in each hand.

The next hand comes from the 1970 World Pairs Olympiad in Stockholm.

♠ 3
♡ A K J 4   *Love all*
♢ 10 3 2   *Dealer West*
♣ A Q 10 6 4

W	N	E	S
1 ♢	2 ♢	3 ♢	3 ♡
—	4 ♡	—	4 NT
—	5 ♡	—	6 ♡
All pass			

♠ A 10 8 7 5
♡ 8 7 6 5 3 2
♢ Q
♣ 9

West leads the seven of diamonds to his partner's ace, and you ruff the return of the eight of diamonds. Trumps are drawn with the ace and king, East discarding the six of diamonds on the second round. How should you continue?

Counting two ruffs in dummy you have ten tricks. The eleventh could come from a club finesse and the twelfth from a 4–3 club break, but there is also the chance of a black suit squeeze if East has five clubs and four spades. If that is the situation East will now be out of diamonds, and you should therefore apply pressure by ruffing the third diamond. If East discards a club, you can lead a club to the ace and ruff out the suit. If East discards a spade, you can establish the spades by ruffing twice in dummy.

You may go wrong, of course, if East discards a spade from a holding of five spades and four clubs. However, East might have mentioned a five-card major in the bidding.

In Stockholm this plan would have worked, for the East–West hands were:

♠ Q J 9   ♠ K 6 4 2
♡ Q 10   ♡ 9
♢ K J 9 7 5 4   ♢ A 8 6
♣ K 2   ♣ J 8 7 5 3

When the third diamond is led East is unable to withstand the pressure.

```
♠ J 7 4 2
♡ 10 3                        N–S game
♢ 4                          Dealer East
♣ Q J 10 8 7 3       W      N        E        S
                                     1 ♢      Dbl
♠ K 8 3              2 ♡    3 ♣      3 ♢      3 NT
♡ A K 6              Dbl    All pass
♢ J 9 6 5
♣ A K 5
```

West leads the ace of diamonds, and even if you dis-
approve of your partner's bidding you have to admire his
nerve in standing the double. East encourages with the eight
of diamonds, but at trick two West switches to the queen of
hearts. East contributes the four of hearts and you win the
trick with the king. When you cash the ace and king of clubs
East shows out on the second round, discarding a diamond.
How should you continue?

The distribution of the cards seems fairly clear. East is
marked with seven diamonds and West is likely to have six
hearts. That leaves East with two hearts and three spades,
which must surely include the ace. Although you have only
eight winners at the moment, the defenders have only four—
three diamonds and the ace of spades. The run of the clubs
will catch East in a strip-squeeze of sorts, and when you
eventually lead a spade from the table he will be bound to
give you a ninth trick either in spades or in diamonds. You
are discarding behind East and need do no more than follow
his discards, coming down to the same number of cards as he
does in spades and diamonds.

There is an important proviso, however. Before running
the rest of the clubs you must cash the ace of hearts. Otherwise you will leave an extra idle card in the East hand and
your hand will be squeezed first. Try it both ways and see the
difference.

♠ 8 6 5 3
♡ Q 10   *Game all*
◇ A K 8 3   *Dealer East*
♣ K 9 5   W   N   E   S
                                       1 ♠   2 ♡
♠ K 7   —   4 ♡   —   —
♡ A K 8 7 3   Dbl   *All pass*
◇ 7 5
♣ A 7 6 2

West leads the two of hearts, and it is not altogether unexpected when East discards the four of diamonds on
dummy's ten. How do you plan the play?

From the discard East appears to have five diamonds. He
is unlikely to have more than five spades, for West would
presumably have led a singleton spade if he had one. You
therefore have five tricks in the side suits, and you will make
the contract if you can score five more from trumps. That
will be possible only if you can manœuvre to ruff your fourth
club with the queen of hearts.

Clearly this is an exercise in avoidance. West must be kept
off lead, for a trump return would ruin your plan. You need
to find a 3-3 club break with East holding at least two of the
three outstanding honour cards in the suit. What is more,
you must tackle the clubs at once to get the timing right. The
correct play is a low club from dummy at trick two. If East
attempts to unblock by playing the queen, you can allow
him to hold the trick. If he plays the knave, the ten or a
small card, however, you should win with the ace and
'finesse' the nine on the way back.

After winning the club or diamond return in dummy you
can lead a spade. East may take his ace and return a spade,
but the timing will be right for your trump coup. Cash the
remaining tops in the minor suits, ruff a spade or a diamond
with the ace of trumps, and ruff your last club with the queen
of trumps. With nothing but trumps left in his hand, West

will have to under-ruff on these two tricks. When you ruff another card with the seven of hearts West will be able to over-ruff with the nine. But he will have to concede the last two tricks to your king and eight.

The distribution you have to play for is shown below.

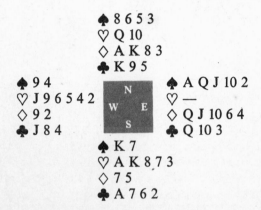

```
                ♠ 8 6 5 3
                ♡ Q 10
                ◇ A K 8 3
                ♣ K 9 5
  ♠ 9 4                          ♠ A Q J 10 2
  ♡ J 9 6 5 4 2        N         ♡ —
  ◇ 9 2          W         E     ◇ Q J 10 6 4
  ♣ J 8 4              S         ♣ Q 10 3
                ♠ K 7
                ♡ A K 8 7 3
                ◇ 7 5
                ♣ A 7 6 2
```

Any other lead would have given you an easier task. On the trump lead the contract cannot be made if spades are tackled before clubs. East will play the ace and another spade, and will return a third spade when given the lead on the second round of clubs. This gives West the opportunity to discard his third club when South ruffs high.

The last hand brings together a number of the points that we have been studying—deductions from bidding and play, counting, avoidance and timing. But the main lesson of the hand, as of the book, is that forethought is the prime ingredient of logical play.